Bob & Joe's
Smart Seafood Guide

A Practical Look at Seafood

By
Bob Marino & Joe D'Alessandro

Published by CATS Publishing, Inc.
442 Route 202-206 North, Suite 274
Bedminster, New Jersey 07921 USA
Phone: 908-781-2589 Fax: 908-781-8598
e-mail: carolyn@net-lynx.com
web site: www.bobandjoes.com

Bob & Joe's Smart Seafood Guide © Copyright 2000 Cats Publishing, Inc., All rights reserved.
Web Site: www.bobandjoes.com
Bob and Joe's Enterprises, Inc.- *Innovative Seafood Concepts*

Library of Congress Catalog Number: 98-74998
ISBN # 09656571-2-4
Printed in the United States of America

Published by CATS Publishing, Inc.
442 Route 202-206 North, Suite 274
Bedminster, NJ 07921 USA
Phone: 908-781-2589 Fax: 908-781-8598 e-mail: carolyn@net-lynx.com
Selected distribution by Gerald F. Antanies, President/CEO Press Media Group, LLC.
Publishers of The Ledger, The Rustburg Villager, The Forest Forum and The North-South Connector
P.O. Box 519, Rustburg, VA. 24588 Phone: 804-332-5728 Fax: 804-332-4895
email: pressmediagroup@world.att.net Web Site: www.theledgeronline.com

Editors: Marcia Schneider, Bob Marino
Book design: Bob Marino, Joe D'Alessandro and Carolyn Schneider
Front and back cover: Ray Sternesky Design, New York, N.Y. 212 226-2707

Recipes and other photos © copyright 2000 All rights reserved by Bob Marino.
Union Oyster House photo © copyright 2000 All rights reserved by Joe D'Alessandro.
Back cover photos courtesy of Fishermen's Grotto, California, Sydney Fish Market, Australia,
Tsukiji Fish Market - Japan National Tourist Organization, Billingsgate Fish Market, England.

Select photos courtesy of: Sydney Fish Market- Australia, Tsukiji Fish Market and Japan National Tourist
Organization, Japan, Rungis Market- France, Hong Kong Fish Market- China, Fulton Fish Market- New
York, Philadelphia Fish Market and Italian Market- Pennsylvania, Atlantic Mussel Growers- Prince Edward
Island, Canada, Nature's Catch- Clarksdale, Mississippi, Southern Pride Catfish- Greensboro, Alabama,
Clear Springs Foods- Buhl, Idaho, Rain Forest Aquaculture- Canas, Costa Rica, Citarella- New York,
New York, Marino's Fine Foods- Springfield, New Jersey, Catfish Cafe- Lynbrook, New York, Sansom
Street Oyster House- Philadelphia, Pennsylvania, Marino's Grand Fish Market, Long Island City, New
York, City Crab Restaurant- New York, New York, Cafe Palermo- New York, New York, Union Oyster
House- Boston, Massachusetts, Fishermen's Grotto- San Francisco, Ca., Pike Place Market, Seattle, Wa.,
Shoal Harbor- Belford, New Jersey, Mansueto's- Watchung, N.J., Caviarteria- New York, New York

Other fine publications by CATS Publishing include *The Ultimate Consignment & Thrift Store Guide*, an
international guide to the world's best consignment, thrift, vintage & secondhand stores.
Web Site: www.consignmentguide.com

Thanks to Jane Lakritz, Maryann Guinan, Gussie Cotroneo, Nancy Dimino and Rick Geraldi for their help.

Dedicated to all seafood lovers
and
seafood lovers to be.

Many thanks to our family, friends and associates
for their encouragement and support.

A very special note of thanks to:
Bob O'Brien, Consumer Advocate
Joe Franklin, The King of Nostalgia
Edward and Pat Kriso
and
Richie Ornstein
for their support and friendship.

TABLE OF CONTENTS

A Note to our Readers

After spending many years working in the seafood industry, we wanted to share our knowledge and expertise with consumers. Exciting facts, delicious recipes and fascinating tidbits about seafood await you in Bob and Joe's Smart Seafood Guide.

For extra visual flavor, we have selected pictures of old-fashioned and current seafood markets from around the world. Many photos capture the essence of market life as it existed many years ago and how it appears today.

While technology has changed over the years, the basic philosophy of carefully selecting, preparing and enjoying delicious seafood remains the same. We hope you enjoy reading this book as much as we have enjoyed writing it.

Bob Marino and Joe D'Alessandro

Smart Seafood Purchasing Tips

- Fresh seafood should appear moist and vibrant in color.

- Fresh seafood must be refrigerated or displayed on ice.

- Raw and cooked seafood should be displayed separately to prevent cross contamination.

- Check to see that cut seafood (flesh) is not in direct contact with ice.

- Previously frozen seafood should be labeled as such.

- Frozen seafood lasts several months when stored in an airtight package.

- Ask your seafood market if the fillets you are purchasing are boneless.

- Check all frozen seafood carefully. Look for packages that are sealed tightly and check for freezer burn.

- Check all labels and dates on packaged seafood for ingredient listings and freshness.

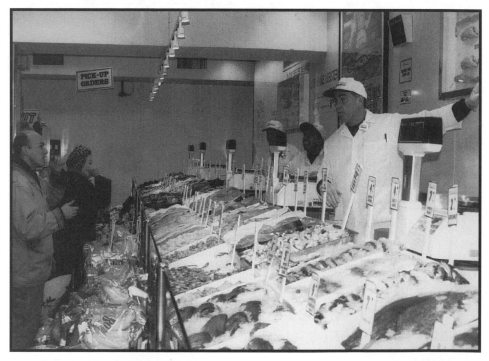

Citarella gourmet markets in Manhattan offers a wide variety of fresh fish on ice and freshly prepared seafood specialties.

*Many seafood markets provide additional
time-saving services which include cleaning shrimp,
opening clams and steaming live lobster.*

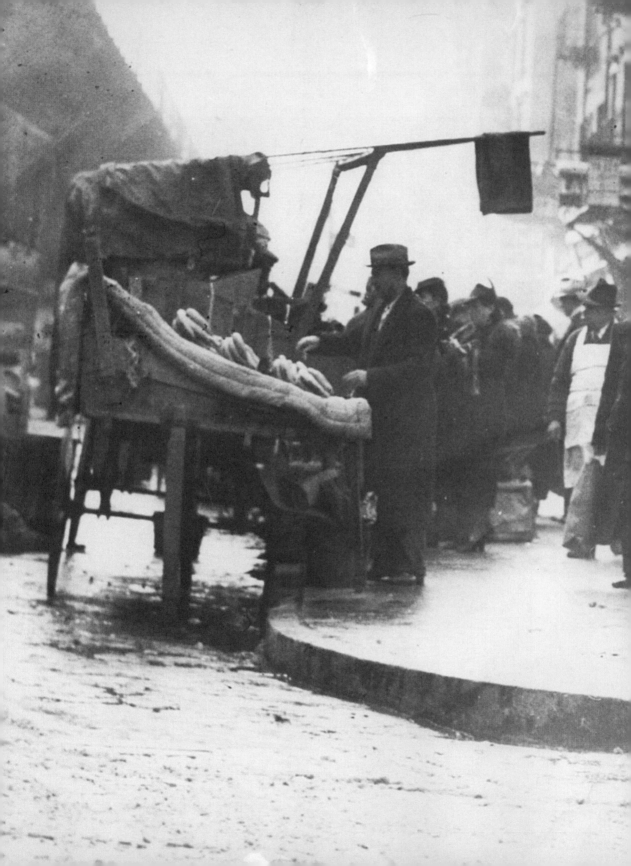

Smart Seafood Storage & Handling Tips

Photo courtesy of the Sydney Fish Market

● After purchasing seafood, refrigerate as soon as possible. Freeze seafood that is not consumed within 48 hours. Before freezing, rinse seafood with cold tap water.

● With the exception of live shellfish, fresh seafood should be stored in an airtight package in the refrigerator.

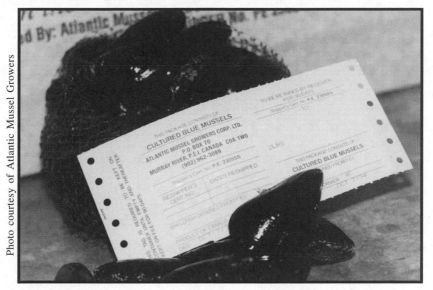

Photo courtesy of Atlantic Mussel Growers

Retail seafood markets are required by law to retain shellfish documentation. This ensures freshness and guarantees the product was harvested from certified waters.

● The safest way to defrost seafood is in your refrigerator.

● A quick way to defrost seafood is to fill a bowl with luke warm tap water. Place seafood in a sealed plastic bag inside bowl to thaw.

● Date all seafood packages before storing in freezer.

● Do not refreeze seafood.

● Wash your hands, counters, utensils and cutting boards with hot soapy water before and after preparing seafood.

● If you are doubtful about the freshness of a seafood product, discard it.

Seafood Favorites

Photo courtesy of Natures Catch

Farm-raised bass harvested in Mississippi.

Bluefish

Fishermen follow the migration of bluefish from the Gulf of Mexico to Maine because it is as enjoyable to catch as it is to eat. With its distinct full flavor and tender texture, bluefish is a delicious tasting fish.

Bluefish is a great source of omega-3 oils which help lower cholesterol levels. Reasonably priced, bluefish can easily be prepared by grilling, broiling or baking.

Smart Tip

● Bluefish that range from 1 to 2 lbs. are referred to as snapper blues. Small snapper blues are milder in taste, firmer in texture and less oily than larger bluefish.

Culinary Tips

● When grilling, place fillets on foil to prevent from falling through grates.

● Before preparing bluefish, submerge fillets in milk for 30 minutes. Rinse with cold tap water. This reduces the oil level in bluefish and sweetens its taste.

Grilled Bluefish

2 lbs. bluefish fillets
2 cups milk
Juice from 1 fresh lemon
1/4 teaspoon garlic powder
1/2 teaspoon oregano
1/4 teaspoon black pepper
4 tablespoons butter
2 tablespoons olive oil
1/2 teaspoon parsley

Rinse bluefish fillets under cold tap water and let drain.
Submerge fillets in milk and refrigerate for 30 minutes.

Melt butter. In a shallow dish combine butter, oil, lemon,
garlic, oregano, pepper and parsley. Remove fillets from
milk. Rinse again with water and place into lemon/butter
marinade.

Preheat grill, on medium to high heat. Wrap fillets in foil.
Cook 15-20 minutes on closed grill or until fish flakes
easily with a fork.

Serves 4

Accompaniments:
corn-on-the-cob
cole slaw (See page 171.)

Catfish

Photo courtesy of Southern Pride Catfish

A meticulously cultivated catfish pond in Alabama

Catfish is the most abundant farm-raised fish in the U.S.
Raised in fresh water ponds throughout the southern United
States, catfish reach their market size of 1-2 pounds in 18
months. Alabama, Arkansas, Louisiana and Mississippi are
the world's leading producers of farmed catfish.

Catfish is available as fillets, nuggets, strips or whole.
Extremely versatile, farmed catfish offers a mild, sweet
taste with a white flaky texture. Low in fat and high in protein,
catfish is delicious fried, sauted, broiled or grilled. For a
unique and delicious taste, try it blackened. (See page 17.)

Smart Tips

● Pristine water conditions and a healthy grain based diet make farm-raised catfish a consistently sweet and delicious fish.

● Fresh catfish fillets, nuggets and strips should appear moist and whitish pink in color.

*The **Catfish Cafe** located in Lynbrook, N.Y., specializes in award winning catfish cuisine.*

Catfish harvested at a farm in Greensboro, Alabama

Within hours after harvesting, farmed catfish is processed, packaged and shipped to markets around the world.

Blackened Catfish

2 lbs. catfish fillets
1 stick butter
1/4 cup cajun or crab seasoning

Rinse catfish fillets under cold water and let drain. Preheat a large skillet. Melt butter. Dip fillets into butter.

Lightly cover fillets with seasoning. Place fillets in hot skillet and cook 2-3 minutes on each side or until fish flakes easily with a fork.

Serves 4

Accompaniments:
white rice
string beans

Culinary Tip

- Add remaining butter/spices to white rice.

Caviar

Photo courtesy of Caviarteria

Known as a delicacy around the world, caviar is the processed roe (eggs) of sturgeon. Russia has long been the leading producer of the finest sturgeon caviar in the world. Other popular varieties found in the United States include salmon, trout, and whitefish caviars.

American Caviars

The flavor of American sturgeon caviar varies from slightly salty to deliciously nutty. Although American sturgeon caviar is smaller in size, it is often compared to Russian sevruga caviar. Similar in flavor and appearance, American sturgeon caviar offers a cost savings.

Other American caviars include salmon and trout, which are known for their reddish-orange color, large size and robust flavor. Golden whitefish caviar is small in size and offers a mild taste.

Russian Caviars

Beluga

Russian beluga caviar is considered to be the finest and most expensive caviar in the world. Its color varies from slate to dark gray and offers a light salty, buttery flavor. Beluga offers the largest eggs and is best enjoyed with points of toast and champagne.

Oscetra

Visually appealing, Russian oscetra caviar color ranges from light to dark brown. Its sweet, almond flavor makes this caviar extremely versatile. It is delicious layered on smoked trout, fresh oysters and more.

Sevruga

Sevruga caviar is the smallest and least expensive of the Russian caviars. Ranging in color from light to dark gray, sevruga is intense in flavor. Sevruga is the perfect accompaniment to smoked salmon with a touch of sour cream.

Caviarteria with locations in Manhattan, Beverly Hills, Las Vegas and Miami specializes in fine caviar from around the world.

Smart Tips

● Fresh caviar is highly perishable and typically lasts 7-10 days unopened in the refrigerator. After it is opened, it should be consumed within 48 hours.

● For cost savings purchase partially broken or pressed sturgeon eggs.

● The term "malassol" on the label means the caviar contains a light salt content and is high quality.

● Patronize only reputable markets for quality caviar at competitive prices.

Avoid using silverware when serving caviar. Mother of pearl spoons will preserve caviar's natural delicious flavor.

Photo courtesy of Citarella

Chilean Sea Bass

Known as "cod of the deep", the average Chilean sea bass weighs 20 lbs. However, records indicate that Chilean sea bass may grow to over 100 lbs.

Rich in omega-3 oils and mild in flavor, prepared Chilean sea bass is moist and delicious. Excellent grilled, baked or pan seared.

Smart Tips

● Chilean sea bass fillets should appear moist and snow white.

● Fall through early Spring is the best time to purchase Chilean sea bass because of availability.

Grilled Chilean Sea Bass

2 lbs. Chilean sea bass fillets
4 oz. honey teriyaki marinade

Rinse fillets under cold tap water and drain. Cut fillets into 4-6 oz. portions.

Brush grate with oil. Preheat grill on medium to high heat. Completely cover fillets with honey teriyaki. Place fillets on grill. Cook fillets approximately 8 minutes on each side, turning once until fillets flake easily with a fork. Continue to baste while grilling.

Serves 4

Accompaniments:
grilled asparagus
grilled red skinned potatoes

Culinary Tips

• Alternative: Pan seared Chilean sea bass - Heat 2 tablespoons olive oil in a skillet. Sprinkle bass to taste with crab seasoning. Sear 2 minutes on each side. Place bass in oven-safe baking dish and bake in 350 degree oven for approximately 8-10 minutes.

• The high oil content in Chilean sea bass helps it stay moist even after extensive cooking.

Clams

The sweet taste and tender texture of clams makes them an appealing choice. Available year round, clams are found in certified waters which are closely monitored by the U.S. Government for pollution control. Some areas in the U.S. that commercially produce clams include Connecticut, Florida, Long Island, New England, New Jersey, Virginia and Washington State.

The supply, quality and price of clams is determined by water temperatures and overall weather conditions. Clams traditionally are more plentiful and reasonably priced during warmer months.

Several varieties of hard shell clams include littlenecks, cherrystones and chowders. Hard shell clams are sold according to size. High in protein, clams taste delicious on the half shell and prepared in chowders, cioppinos or paellas.

Caught along the Atlantic coast, soft-shell clams are oval shaped with a long soft neck. Soft shell clams are often referred to as "steamers". Steamers are best when served with broth and melted butter.

Smart Tips

● Clams open naturally to breathe. Avoid purchasing open clams that do not close when tapped lightly.

● Hard-shell and soft-shell clams should be kept at consistently cool temperatures (48 degrees fahrenheit). After purchasing clams, refrigerate as soon as possible.

● Manila and cockle clams are smaller in size than littleneck clams and are a delicious addition to pasta dishes.

● Topneck clams are hard-shell clams which are slightly larger than littlenecks.

● Mahogany clams resemble littlenecks but are a different species. With their darker shell, mahogany clams are less expensive than littlenecks and are tasty in chowders and cioppinos.

Clams harvested at a farm in Cedar Key, Florida

Steamer Clams with Broth & Butter

4 lbs. soft-shell steamer clams
2 1/2 cups water
1 small onion, cut into quarters
1 cup sliced carrots
3 sliced celery sticks
1 stick butter

Rinse clams under cold tap water. Pour water in a large pot. Add onions, sliced carrots and celery sticks. Bring to a boil. Add steamer clams and cover.

Cook approximately 6-8 minutes until clams open. Save a portion of broth and place in a serving bowl. Melt butter and place into separate bowl. Dip steamer clams in broth then melted butter.

Serves 2

Steamed Clams with Melted Butter

2 dozen littleneck or cherrystone clams
1 stick butter
Juice from 1 fresh lemon
1 tablespoon parsley
1/4 teaspoon black pepper

Place 1/2 inch of water in a large pot. Add clams, and cover. Allow clams to steam approximately 8-12 minutes or until they open. Discard any clams that do not open.
Melt butter. Stir in lemon, parsley and black pepper. Place clams on serving dish and serve with melted butter mixture.
Serves 2

Culinary Tip

● Clams open easily when cooked on an outdoor grill.

Cod

For centuries, cod has been a culinary favorite. Found in the Atlantic and Pacific Oceans, cod offers a mild sweet taste and flaky texture.

Cod is available fresh or frozen. State of the art equipment allows fishermen to process, package, and freeze cod on their vessels immediately after it is caught. Cod is then distributed to the market frozen or thawed.

High in protein and low in fat, cod is a perfect ingredient in fish cakes and chowders. Cod tastes delicious sauteed, baked, fried or broiled.

Smart Tip

● Cod range in weight from 2 to 25 lbs. Smaller cod weighing 1 1/2 - 2 lbs. are referred to as "scrod".

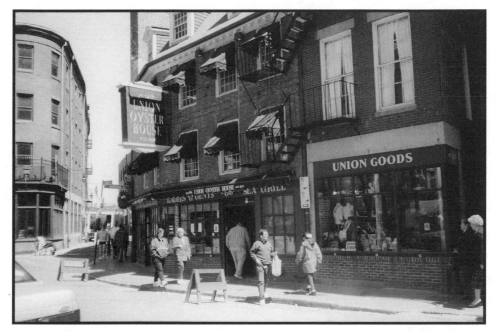

*The famous **Union Oyster House** in Boston, Massachusetts features flavorful seafood dishes. Cod, flounder and lobster are among the top seafood specialties prepared to gourmet perfection at this historic restaurant.*

Baked Cod Marinara

2 lbs. cod fillets
16 oz. marinara sauce
2 tablespoons parmesan cheese
1/4 teaspoon black pepper
1/2 cup mozzarella cheese

Preheat oven to 350 degrees. Rinse cod under cold tap water and let drain. In an oven-safe baking dish, cover fillets completely with marinara sauce. Sprinkle lightly with black pepper and parmesan cheese. Cover fillets with foil and bake for 12 to 15 minutes. Remove from oven, add shredded mozzarella cheese and bake for an additional 5 minutes or until cheese melts and fish flakes easily with a fork.

Serves 4

Accompaniments:
garden salad
sauteed escarole

Culinary Tip

● The tail portion of cod fillet is best prepared by sauteing or broiling. The thicker section of cod fillet tastes best baked or fried.

Soft-Shell Blue Crab

Soft-shell crabs are most plentiful along the southeastern coastline of the United States during the Spring and Summer months.

Soft-shell crabs are available in a variety of sizes which are graded and priced accordingly, based on size. Crabs grow by shedding their outer shell.

After shedding, the entire crab softens and becomes edible.

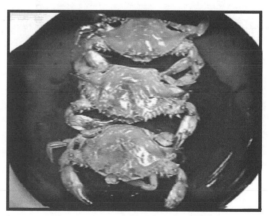

Fresh soft-shell crabs are available during warmer months. Frozen soft-shell crabs are available year round.

Smart Tips

● Soft-shell crabs taste best fried or sauted.

● For easier preparation, ask your seafood market to clean soft-shell crabs.

Soft-Shell Crab

4 jumbo soft-shell crabs
5 eggs
2 cups Italian seasoned bread crumbs
1 cup flour
1 cup vegetable oil

Rinse soft-shell crabs and let drain. Pour flour into a bowl.
In a separate bowl, beat eggs. Pour seasoned bread
crumbs into a separate shallow dish. Cover each crab completely with flour. Shake off excess flour. Dip crabs into
egg. Cover with bread crumbs.

In a large frying pan, heat oil on high heat. Place crabs into
frying pan and cook approximately 4 minutes on each side
or until golden brown.

Serve with cocktail, tartar or hot sauce and fresh lemon.

Serves 4

Accompaniments:
oven fried chips (See page 163.)
cole slaw (See page 171.)

Manhattan's **City Crab Restaurant** *specializes in a large selection of delicious crab dishes including their famous sauteed soft-shell crab.*

Hard Shell Blue Crabs

Blue Crab Meat

Blue crab meat is available in various grades and classified according to size. Ranging from the largest to smallest they include jumbo lump, backfin, special and claw meat.

Crab meat is hand or machine picked. It is available fresh or pasteurized at local markets. Pasteurized crab meat is processed and packaged which allows for an extended shelf life. Fresh crab meat should be consumed within several days after purchasing.

Cocktail claws (fingers) are scored sections of the crab's claws. Cocktail claws make excellent hors d' oeuvres.

Smart Tip

● Another member of the crab family is the swimmer crab. Imported from Asia, the meat from the swimmer crab is similar in appearance to blue crab but less flavorful.

Steamed Crabs

2 dozen live crabs
1/2 cup crab spice
3 cups water

Place two dozen live crabs into a large pot of boiling water.
Sprinkle with crab spice. Cook 12-15 minutes, covered.

Crabs will turn bright reddish-orange when fully cooked.
Remove crabs from pot and place in refrigerator to cool.

Serves 4

*Hard-shell blue
crabs are
available live,
cooked or frozen.
Steaming live
crabs enhances
their flavor to the
fullest.*

King Crab

King crab makes its home in the northern waters of the Pacific Ocean, near Alaska and Russia. The most popular varieties of king crab include red and golden. Red king crab is considered to be more flavorful.

King crab, the largest member of the crab family, is best known for its sweet and succulent flavor. The average king crab weighs10 lbs. Most of the edible meat comes from the crab's legs and claws.

Smart Tip

● Avoid purchasing king crab that appears dehydrated or faded in color.

Culinary Tip

● Serve king crab with melted butter or cocktail sauce and fresh lemon.

Snow Crab

Snow crab is seasonally caught in the northern Pacific and Atlantic Oceans, predominately off the coast of Alaska and Canada.

Snow crab has a sweet, succulent taste and is available as cooked claws and clusters. Claws are best suited for hors d'oeuvres. Snow crab clusters taste delicious served as a main course with melted butter. Snow crab meat makes a delightful addition to salads, sauces and stuffings.

Photo courtesy of Spingarn Corp.

An Alaskan fishing boat heading out to sea in search of crab.

Smart Tip

● The best time to purchase snow crab is March through June when it is most plentiful.

Snow Crab with Honey Mustard Sauce

2 lbs. cooked snow crab claws
1 (9 oz.) jar honey mustard
1 tablespoon sour cream
1 teaspoon horseradish

Thaw cooked snow crab claws overnight in refrigerator. Rinse lightly under cold tap water.

In a bowl, combine honey mustard, sour cream and horseradish. Mix thoroughly until creamy. Serve snow crab claws with honey mustard sauce.
Serves 4

Culinary Tip

● The taste of snow crab is enhanced by lightly rinsing the outer shell under cold tap water before preparing. This reduces the amount of natural salt left on the crab.

For a simple and delicious meal, serve snow crab with melted butter.

Stone Crab Claws

Stone crabs are caught along the southern Atlantic coast. Available fresh or frozen, stone crabs are harvested solely for their claws. After they are caught, the stone crab claws are removed. The crabs are placed back into the water and their claws regenerate.

Stone crab claw meat is sweet and firm in texture. Traditionally, stone crab claws are served with hot mustard sauce, cocktail sauce or melted butter.

Smart Tip

● The best time of year to purchase stone crabs is October through May when they are abundant.

Dungeness Crab

Indigenous to the northern Pacific coast of the United States and Canada, dungeness crab is rich and sweet in flavor. Dungeness crab is available live, fresh or frozen.

Low in fat and calories and high in protein, dungeness crab tastes best steamed and served with lemon and melted butter.

Fishermen's Grotto in San Francisco is famous for fresh dungeness crab which is served in abundance.

Smart Tip

● The best time of year to purchase dungeness crab is December and January because of availability.

San Francisco Style Dungeness Crab

4 dungeness crabs
1 large pot of water
1/4 cup salt
2 cups oil-based Italian salad dressing

Boil a large pot of water. Add salt. Place crabs in water, covering completely. Boil approximately 18 to 20 minutes. Remove crabs from pot and cool in refrigerator.

Remove back shell and rinse crab with cold tap water. In a bowl, combine crab with salad dressing and let marinate several hours in refrigerator.

Serves 4

Culinary Tip

● Dungeness crab meat tastes delicious added to marinara sauce and served over pasta.

Jonah Crab

Found in deep water off the coast of New England, jonah crab is a healthy and delicious crab alternative. Jonah crab is more commonly found in New England seafood markets. Jonah crab can be used in many recipes including dips, chowders, stuffings and quiches.

Crab Quiche

1/2 cup mayonnaise
2 eggs
2 tablespoons flour
1/2 cup milk
8 oz. chopped jonah crab meat
8 oz. swiss cheese, diced
1/3 cup chopped scallions
1/2 tablespoon dried parsley
1 frozen 9 inch pie shell

In a bowl, combine mayonnaise, flour, eggs and milk. Mix until blended.

Pour into nine inch round pie shell. Mix crab meat, cheese, parsley and chopped scallions. Pour into pie shell. Bake at 350 degrees for 45 minutes.

Serves 6-8

Crawfish

Sweet and delicious, crawfish is caught in Louisiana waters. Crawfish is a long-time favorite in Louisiana. Crawfish is also imported into the U.S. from Asia.

Similar to lobster and shrimp in taste and texture, crawfish is a perfect complement to creoles, paellas, chowders and cioppinos.

Smart Tips

● Spring is the best time to purchase crawfish because of availability.

● Crawfish tail meat may be substituted for shrimp and lobster in many recipes.

Sauted Crawfish

1 1/2 lbs. cooked crawfish meat
2 cups white rice
1/2 cup chicken broth
2 cloves chopped garlic
1/2 stick butter
2 tablespoons olive oil
1/4 cup chopped onion
1/2 cup fresh mushrooms
2 1/2 teaspoons cajun
  seasoning or 1/2 teaspoon
  each of white pepper,
  black pepper, cayenne
  pepper, dried oregano, basil

Cook rice according to package directions. Set aside and keep warm. Melt butter and olive oil in large skillet. Add onions and garlic. Saute several minutes until soft. Add crawfish, mushrooms, chicken broth, seasonings and butter. Saute an additional 4-6 minutes, stirring frequently. Place rice in serving dish. Pour crawfish and sauce over rice.

Serves 4

Culinary Tip

● Alternative: Live crawfish may be prepared by boiling water seasoned with crawfish/crab spice. Place crawfish in water. After water returns to a boil, cook for one minute and remove from heat. Leave crawfish in water for an additional 10 minutes to absorb spicy seasoning.

Flounder

Known for its light delicate texture and mild flavor, flounder is a favorite throughout the world. Flounder is caught along the Atlantic and Pacific coasts of the United States and Canada.

Some of the most common varieties of flounder include:

European Dover Sole
Blackback
Fluke
Gray Sole
Pacific Dover Sole
Petrale Sole
Rex Sole
Rock Sole
Sea Dab
Turbot
Yellowtail

Smart Tip

● Fresh flounder fillets vary in color from white to light gray. Flounder turns white when cooked.

Flounder Francais

2 lbs. flounder fillets
1 cup flour
3 eggs
1 stick butter
1 tablespoon olive oil
Juice from 2 fresh lemons
1/2 teaspoon black pepper
1/4 teaspoon garlic powder
1 teaspoon fresh chopped parsley

Rinse flounder under cold water and let drain. In a mixing bowl combine flour, black pepper and garlic powder. Beat eggs in a separate bowl. Cover fillets with flour mixture. Dip into egg mixture and again in flour.

Melt butter and olive oil in a skillet. Add lemon juice. Place fillets in skillet and saute 3-4 minutes on each side or until fillets flake easily with a fork. Garnish with parsley.

Accompaniments:
spinach
risotto

Serves 4

Flounder cut into fillets at the Fulton Fish Market.

Grouper

Grouper is found in warm tropical waters around the world. The most common varieties of grouper are red and black. Both varieties share a sweet and distinctive taste. Its white appearance and lean texture add to its appeal and make it excellent for grilling, baking or broiling.

Fresh grouper unloaded from a fishing boat in Central America.

Smart Tip

● Summer and Fall are the best times of the year to purchase grouper because of availability.

Broiled Grouper

2 lbs. grouper fillets
1/3 cup melted butter
1/4 teaspoon paprika
4 tablespoons extra fine cracker meal
1 tablespoon parmesan cheese
1/4 teaspoon garlic powder
1/2 teaspoon dried parsley

Rinse fillets under cold tap water and let drain. Melt butter.
Dip fillets into melted butter. Place fillets on broiler pan
covered with foil. Sprinkle fillets lightly with paprika.

Mix cracker meal, parmesan cheese and garlic powder
together in a separate bowl. Sprinkle mixture over fillets.
Preheat broiler and cook approximately 8-10 minutes or until
fillets flake easily with a fork.

Serves 4

Accompaniments:
baked potato
grilled zucchini   **Culinary Tips**

● Due to its low fat content, grouper tends to become dry
when overcooked.

● Grouper is exceptional in fish chowders or cioppinos.

Haddock

An elite member of the cod family, haddock is caught throughout the north Atlantic Ocean and found in abundance along the New England coast. Haddock is imported into the U.S. from Norway, Russia, Iceland and Canada.

High in protein and low in fat, haddock has a lean, white flaky texture. Mild in flavor, haddock is delicious fried, sauted or baked.

Smart Tip

● Haddock fillet is customarily sold with skin intact to distinguish it from less expensive cod.

Baked Haddock

2 lbs. haddock fillets
1 stick butter
Juice from 2 fresh lemons
1/4 teaspoon paprika
2 tablespoons parmesan cheese
1/2 cup extra fine cracker meal
Salt and pepper to taste

Rinse haddock under cold tap water and drain. In a shallow dish, mix parmesan cheese and cracker meal. Melt butter. Baste fillets with butter and place on baking pan. Lightly sprinkle cracker meal mixture and paprika over fillets. Add salt and pepper to taste. Preheat oven and bake for approximately 15 minutes at 375 degrees or until fillets flake easily with a fork.

Serves 4

Accompaniments:
boiled potato
escarole

Culinary Tip

●   Haddock's appealing flaky texture and mild taste make it an ideal ingredient in fish cakes, cioppinos, chowders and the classic "fish and chips".

Halibut

Halibut is the largest member of the flounder family. Caught along the Atlantic and Pacific coasts of the United States and Canada, halibut range in size from 10 to over 100 lbs.

Known for its firm texture and mild flavor, halibut is available as steaks or fillets. Halibut steak tastes delicious baked or grilled. Fillets are best suited for broiling or sauteing.

Smart Tip

● Halibut fillets are not as readily available as steaks therefore ordering fillets in advance is recommended.

Spicy Blackened Halibut

2 lbs. halibut fillets
1 stick butter
1 tablespoon paprika
1/2 teaspoon each of cayenne pepper, black pepper,
  garlic powder and dried oregano
1 tablespoon dried parsley
1 tablespoon olive oil

Rinse halibut fillets under cold tap water and drain. In a small bowl, combine paprika, black pepper, garlic powder, parsley, oregano and cayenne pepper. Melt butter. Dip fillets into melted butter and then into seasonings.

Preheat skillet with oil. Place fillets in hot skillet and cook 2-3 minutes on each side until fish blackens and flakes easily with a fork.

Serves 4

Accompaniments:
wild rice
string beans

Lobster

Lobster is a classic American dish that evokes many happy memories of Summer. The sweet and tender taste of lobster adds to its popularity. The two varieties of lobster include the American and the spiny.

American lobsters are caught off the Atlantic coast. The majority are found in the cold waters of New England, Nova Scotia and New Foundland. The most popular sizes range from 1 to 3 lbs.

The American lobster sheds its shell (molting) in late summer. During the molting season, lobsters generally contain less meat and are referred to as "new shells".

American lobster

Unlike the American lobster, the spiny lobster has no claws. The spiny lobster is caught in both cold and warm waters. Cold water spiny lobsters are caught primarily off the coast of South Africa, New Zealand and Australia. Warm water spiny lobsters are caught from Southern Florida to Brazil.

Spiny lobsters range in size from 1 to 5 lbs. The tail of the spiny lobster is graded by size. Larger tails are more expensive.

Smart Tips

● Spring and Summer are the best time to purchase live American lobster because of availability.

● American live lobsters yield approximately 1/4 pound of edible meat from a one pound lobster.

● Langostinos are small members of the lobster family. Caught in Chilean waters, langostinos are sweet and delicious. Available as frozen cooked tail meat.

Culinary Tips

● The amount of cooking time needed for live lobsters depends upon the size of the lobster. Larger lobsters require more cooking time.

● After cooking live lobster, place in the refrigerator to cool. This will prevent meat from sticking to shell.

● Remove tails and claws from cooked lobster. To remove meat from lobster, place towel over claws and tap lightly with a small hammer until shell cracks. Use sharp shears to cut shell of lobster tail lengthwise and remove meat.

● Steaming and boiling are the recommended methods for cooking live American lobsters. Lobster tails are best prepared by baking or broiling.

Live lobsters are graded according to size. Lobsters that weigh 1 to 1 1/8 lbs. are classified as "chix".

Steamed Lobsters

4 (1 1/4 lb.) live lobsters
1/4 cup white vinegar
1 quart water

Place live lobsters and vinegar into boiling water. Cover pot.
Cook approximately 10 minutes. Lobsters will turn bright
red when done. Allow to cool in refrigerator.

Serve with melted butter and lemon.

Serves 4

Accompaniments:
corn-on-the-cob
oriental seafood salad (See page 179.)

Broiled Lobster Tails

4 (8 oz.) lobster tails
1 stick butter
1/2 cup extra fine cracker meal
1/4 teaspoon each of paprika, garlic powder
2 tablespoons parmesan cheese

Place lobster tails, hard shell side up on cutting board. On meat side, cut hard shell with sharp shears. Avoid cutting meat. With a sharp knife, cut tail meat in half but not completely through. Carefully open lobster tail to expose meat.

Place tails (meat side up) on broiler pan. Melt butter. Set aside. In a separate bowl, mix cracker meal, garlic powder, and parmesan cheese.

Sprinkle lobster tails lightly with paprika. Pour melted butter over lobster tails. Sprinkle with cracker meal mixture. Broil 8-10 minutes or until lobster meat loses its glassy shine.

Serves 4

Accompaniments:
wild rice
zucchini

Culinary Tip

● Lemon ice is a refreshing, palatable dessert, perfect after lobster.

Lemon Ice

1 cup fresh squeezed lemon juice, strained
3/4 cup granulated sugar
1 3/4 cup water

Pour lemon juice and water into a small pot. Heat for approximately one minute. Add sugar. Stir continuously and bring to a boil.

Remove from heat and let cool to room temperature. Pour into small metal or plastic container. Place in freezer for several hours until frozen.

Mackeral

The most popular varieties of mackeral include the Atlantic, Spanish, and king mackeral.

Atlantic mackeral (Boston mackeral) is found in the cold waters of the northern Atlantic. Oily and full-flavored, its texture is soft and flaky.

Boston mackeral

Spanish mackeral is caught along the southern Atlantic coast and the Gulf of Mexico. Milder in flavor than the Atlantic and the king mackeral, Spanish mackeral's soft meat becomes firm after cooking.

King mackeral, the largest member of the mackeral family, is found off the coast of Florida and the Gulf of Mexico. Full flavored, king mackeral lends itself to grilling and baking.

All varieties of mackeral contain high amounts of omega-3 oils which make it a healthy and delicious seafood dish.

Culinary Tip

● Mackerel tastes best when prepared in lemon oil marinade or a tomato based sauce.

Mackeral Marinara

2 lbs. mackeral fillets
2 1/2 cups crushed tomatoes
3 cloves finely chopped garlic
1/2 teaspoon fresh ground black pepper
1 1/2 cups sliced mushrooms
2 tablespoons chopped basil
4 tablespoons parmesan cheese

Rinse mackeral fillets under cold tap water and let drain. In a skillet, heat oil and saute garlic until soft. Stir in tomatoes, mushrooms, pepper and basil. Simmer 10-12 minutes.

Place fillets in sauce and cook an additional 8 minutes. Carefully remove fillets from skillet with a spatula and place on serving dish. Spoon additional sauce over fillets.

Serves 4

Accompaniments:
string beans
white rice

Mahi Mahi

Known as "the dolphin fish" in Hawaii, mahi mahi is predominately found in tropical southern waters.
The average mahi mahi weighs 20 lbs.

Available year round as fresh or frozen fillets, mahi mahi's firm flaky flesh and sweet flavor makes it an excellent candidate for pan searing, broiling or grilling.

Smart Tips

● For milder tasting mahi mahi, trim the dark line before cooking.

● Mahi mahi may be substituted in many swordfish or tuna recipes.

Grilled Mahi Mahi

2 lbs. mahi mahi fillets
1 cup olive oil
1 teaspoon black pepper
Juice from 1 fresh lemon

Rinse mahi mahi fillets under cold water and let drain.
Brush grate with oil. Preheat grill on medium to high heat.
In a bowl, combine oil, lemon juice and pepper. Mix well.

Baste fillets with marinade. Place on grill, skin side down,
and cook approximately 8 minutes. Turn fillets over and
baste again. Cook for an additional 8 minutes or until fish
flakes easily with a fork.

Serves 4

Accompaniments:
grilled asparagus / portabello mushrooms
baked potato

Culinary Tip

● When cooking mahi mahi, constantly baste fillets with
marinade to prevent drying.

Monkfish

Known for its delicious white, sweet tail meat, monkfish is predominately caught in northern Atlantic waters. Because of its firm texture, monkfish lends itself to grilling, frying or sauteing. Rich in taste, monkfish is also an excellent addition to chowders or cioppinos.

A buyer inspects fresh monkfish.

Smart Tips

● For easier preparation, ask your seafood market to remove the outer skin of monkfish.

● Spring and Summer are the best time of year to purchase monkfish because of availability.

Monkfish Marsala

2 lbs. monkfish fillets
3/4 cup flour
1/4 cup butter
1/4 cup olive oil
1/4 cup sliced onion
1 clove diced garlic
1 cup sliced mushrooms
1/4 cup marsala wine
3 tablespoons finely chopped parsley

Rinse monkfish under cold tap water and let drain. Cut monkfish into 1/2 inch thick medallions. Place 1/2 cup flour in mixing bowl. Add salt and pepper to taste. Coat fish evenly with flour.

Heat oil and butter in skillet. Add garlic and onions and saute until soft. Place monkfish in skillet and saute approximately 2 minutes on each side. Remove monkfish from skillet. Set aside and keep warm.

Add mushrooms to skillet and saute on low heat for several minutes. Slowly stir in remaining flour to thicken. Add wine and parsley. Let simmer one additional minute. Place monkfish on serving dish and cover with marsala sauce.

Serves 4

Accompaniments:
pasta and garden salad

Mussels

Photo courtesy of Atlantic Mussel Growers

The waters off Prince Edward Island are home to farm-raised blue mussels. It generally takes 2-3 years for farmed mussels to reach their market size.

Farmed off the coast of New Zealand and South America, the green lipped mussel is larger in size than the blue mussel.

Tender, plump and sweet tasting, blue mussels are found along the north Atlantic coast of the U.S. and Canada. High in protein and versatile, mussels are tasty in soups, salads, paellas or pasta dishes. Steaming or sauteing is the best way to prepare blue mussels.

Culinary Tips

● When cooking blue mussels without sauce or marinade, remove from heat as they open. This prevents mussels from drying out.

● Blue mussels taste delicious added to marinara sauce and served over linguine.

● Green lipped mussels taste delicious topped with a butter garlic or marinara sauce and served warm on the half shell.

Sauted Mussels in Lemon Butter

4 lbs. fresh mussels
1 stick of butter
Juice from 1 fresh lemon
1/4 cup white wine or cooking sherry
1 tablespoon parsley
1 clove chopped garlic

Rinse 4 lbs. of live mussels and let drain. In a large skillet over medium heat, melt butter. Add lemon, garlic, white wine and parsley. Simmer 2 minutes stirring occasionally. Add mussels, partially cover skillet.

As mussels open, remove from skillet and place on a platter. Pour butter sauce over mussels and serve hot.

Serves 4

Accompaniments:
Italian bread
Caesar salad

Ocean Perch

Often referred to as rose or red fish because of its bright red skin, ocean perch is found in the cold deep waters of the northern Atlantic. Ocean perch range in weight from 1 to 3 lbs. Available as fillets, ocean perch has a sweet flavor, delicate texture and is best baked, broiled, or sauted.

Sauted Perch

2 lbs. ocean perch fillets
2 tablespoons olive oil
1 stick melted butter
1/2 cup blanched, slivered almonds
Juice from 1 fresh lemon
3/4 cup flour
Salt and pepper to taste

Rinse fillets under cold tap water and drain. Cover fillets with flour that has been seasoned with salt and pepper. In a skillet, heat butter, olive oil, lemon and almonds. Place fillets in skillet and saute for approximately 4 minutes on each side or until fillets flake easily with a fork. Remove fillets from skillet with spatula and place on serving dish. Serves 4

Accompaniments:
string beans
baked potato

Orange Roughy

Caught predominately in deep waters off the coast of New Zealand, Australia and Iceland, orange roughy is primarily processed into fillets and frozen at sea on fishing vessels. Orange roughy has a mild flavor with a flaky white texture. Available fresh or frozen, orange roughy tastes delicious broiled, baked or sauted.

Orange Roughy Milanese

2 lbs. orange roughy fillets
2 tablespoons dried fennel
1 cup Italian bread crumbs
4 eggs
1/4 cup milk
1 cup flour
1 teaspoon black pepper

Rinse orange roughy fillets under cold tap water and drain. In a bowl, mix eggs and milk together. In a separate dish, combine flour and pepper. Set aside.

In another shallow dish, mix together bread crumbs, parmesan cheese and fennel. Completely coat fillets in flour. Dip fillets into egg mixture. Cover with bread crumb mixture.

Coat bottom of skillet with oil and preheat on medium to high heat. Place fillets into skillet and cook for approximately 2 minutes on each side, until golden brown and fish flakes easily with a fork.

Accompaniments:
mashed potatoes
buttered corn

Oysters

Well known for their seductive quality and delicate texture, the taste of oysters vary depending upon their place of origin. Oysters differ in salt content and texture.

Oysters are found in waters around the world. Some popular varieties include the Belon (Maine, France), Blue Point (Long Island, Connecticut), Chatham, (New England) Chincoteague, (Maryland) Kumamoto, (Washington State) and the prized Malpeque (Prince Edward Island).

Oysters are available live in the shell, shucked (taken out of shell), frozen on the half shell, or breaded. Available year round, oysters are high in vitamins, iron and minerals.

Served raw on the half shell, fried, baked, steamed or grilled, oysters are tasty. Perfect for stuffings and stews.

Smart Tip

●   Oysters are most abundant Fall through late Spring.

Oysters On The Grill

20 live oysters in the shell
2 fresh lemons
1/4 cup melted butter
Black pepper to taste

Rinse approximately 20 live oysters in the shell under cold water. Place oysters on a preheated grill. Close grill cover.

Allow approximately 6-8 minutes for oysters to open. After oysters open, remove from grill individually. Serve with melted butter and lemon.

Serves 4

The **Sansom Street Oyster House** in Philadelphia is well
known for their fried oysters served with chicken salad.

Baked Oysters

1 dozen oysters
1/2 cup Italian seasoned bread crumbs
2 tablespoons parmesan cheese
2 tablespoons olive oil
1 tablespoon parsley

Rinse oysters. Wrap oysters in damp paper towels. Microwave on high approximately 1 minute until oysters open slightly. Remove top shell. Place oysters on baking dish.

In a separate dish, combine bread crumbs with parmesan cheese. Spread bread crumb mixture over oysters. Add a dab of olive oil to each oyster.

Place oysters in a preheated 350 degree oven. Bake approximately 10 minutes until brown. Garnish with parsley.

Serves 4

Culinary Tip

● Serve raw oysters on the half shell with fresh lemon, cracked black pepper and a dash of hot sauce.

Rainbow Trout

Available year round, farmed rainbow trout reach their market size in approximately 12 months. They are harvested when their weight reaches 1 to 2 lbs. Larger rainbow trout which resemble salmon are known as "steelhead".

With a soft flaky texture and a mild flavor, rainbow trout are ideal for grilling, broiling or sauteing. Available as fillets and whole fish, rainbow trout is high in protein and contain healthy omega-3 oils.

Photo courtesy of Clear Springs Foods

Idaho is the leading producer of farmed-raised trout in the U.S.

Smart Tip

● When purchasing fresh rainbow trout, flesh should appear moist and firm. Meat color varies from white to bright red.

Sauted Trout

2 lbs. rainbow trout fillet
1/2 cup flour
1 cup milk
2 eggs
1 stick butter
1 tablespoon olive oil
1/4 cup chopped parsley
Juice from 2 fresh lemons
Salt and black pepper to taste

Rinse fillets under cold tap water and let drain. In a mixing bowl combine eggs and milk, mix thoroughly. Dip fillets into egg mixture. In a shallow dish, season flour with salt and pepper. Cover fillets with flour.

In a large skillet, melt butter and oil on medium heat. Add lemon and parsley. Place fillets in skillet and saute approximately 3 minutes on each side until lightly browned. Place fillets on a serving dish and pour remaining sauce over fillets.

Serves 4

Accompaniments:
roasted potatoes
spinach

Red Snapper

Red snapper is known for its delicate texture and distinct, sweet flavor. Caught primarily off the coast of Florida, Brazil and in the Gulf of Mexico, red snapper's average weight is 1-3 lbs. Other members of the snapper family include yellowtail, lane, silk, and vermilion.

Florida red snapper is popular on menus around the world. Low in fat, red snapper is versatile and can be used in many delicious recipes. Pan searing is recommended.

Florida red snapper cut into fillets.

Smart Tips

● The best time to buy red snapper is May through December when they are most plentiful.

● True red snapper fillets are usually sold with skin intact to distinguish it from less expensive snapper.

Pan Seared Red Snapper

2 lbs. red snapper fillets
2 tablespoons wine vinegar
1 tablespoon olive oil
Juice from 1 fresh lemon
1 tablespoon honey
1 teaspoon ground ginger
1/4 cup chopped scallions
1 teaspoon dijon mustard

Rinse red snapper fillets under cold tap water and drain. In a small bowl, combine rice wine vinegar, olive oil, scallions, honey, ground ginger and dijon mustard. Mix until smooth.

Dip fillets in mixture, coating evenly. Place fillets into preheated skillet and cook 2-3 minutes on each side on medium heat. Add remaining sauce, lower heat and simmer an additional 3 minutes or until fish flakes easily with a fork. Place fillets on serving dish with a spatula.

Serves 4

Accompaniments:
risotto
buttered corn

Salmon

Salmon's great taste and positive health benefits make it a popular seafood choice. It is one of the most highly consumed fish in the world.

Rich in omega-3 oils, salmon is found in both the Atlantic and Pacific Oceans. Pacific varieties of wild salmon include red sockeye, silver coho, king, chum and pink. West coast varieties are most abundant May through September.

Farmed Atlantic salmon is available year round and produced in Canada, Chile, Iceland, Ireland, Norway, Scotland and the United States.

Salmon is a healthy, tasty and versatile fish. Grilling, baking, sauteing or broiling is recommended.

Smart Tip

● Fat content in salmon varies. Farm-raised Atlantic salmon, Pacific sockeye, coho and king contain a higher fat content which helps retain moistness after cooking. Pink and chum salmon contain a lower fat content which result in a drier texture after cooking.

Spicy Grilled Salmon

2 lbs. salmon fillets
4 tablespoons olive oil
1/4 cup lemon juice
1/2 tablespoon cayenne pepper
Black pepper to taste

Rinse salmon fillets under cold tap water and let drain. Brush grate with oil. Preheat grill on medium to high heat. In a bowl, combine olive oil, lemon juice and cayenne pepper. Baste salmon fillets with marinade. Place fillets skin side up on grill. Cook approximately 15 minutes, turning once or until fish flakes easily with a fork. Remove from grill with spatula.

Serves 4
Accompaniments:
grilled asparagus
grilled red skinned potatoes

Culinary Tip

● Pink and chum salmon taste delicious cooked whole on the grill or in a mayonnaise-based salad. (See page 181.)

Scallops

Sea, bay and calico are three of the most popular varieties of scallops found in waters around the world.

Because of their large size, delicate texture and mild flavor, sea scallops are ideal for grilling, frying or broiling. Smaller in size, bay and calico scallops are delicious in pasta and rice dishes. Bay and calico scallops are sweet tasting and are best sauted, broiled or fried. Scallops are perfect additions to soups, cioppinos and paellas.

Smart Tips

● Fresh sea scallops vary in color from creamy white to pale orange. Color differences do not affect flavor.

● Before cooking large sea scallops, slice into 1/2 to 3/4 inch thick medallions. This will help scallops cook evenly.

fresh sea scallops

After scallops are harvested, the meat is removed from the shell and packaged (fresh or frozen) on scallop boats.

Broiled Sea Scallops

2 lbs. sea scallops
1/2 stick butter
1/4 cup Italian seasoned
   bread crumbs
Juice from 1 fresh lemon
1 tablespoon parsley
1/2 teaspoon garlic
   powder, paprika

Rinse scallops in cold water and drain in colander. Melt
butter in saucepan or microwave and add lemon juice.
Add parsley and garlic powder, stir.

Place scallops in oven-safe cooking dish. Pour butter
sauce over scallops. Sprinkle lightly with bread crumbs and
paprika. Place in preheated broiler. Cook 6-8 minutes or
until scallops lose their glassy shine. Do not overcook.
Serve over fresh spinach and top with slices of red onion.

Serves 4

Accompaniments:
asparagus
boiled potato

Shrimp

More shrimp are harvested worldwide than any other seafood item. Most domestic shrimp are found in warm waters along the southern United States, from the Carolinas to Texas. Shrimp are imported into the United States from Asia, Central and South America, India and Canada. Shrimp are categorized by color and size. Several popular varieties include pinks, whites, browns and black tigers.

Southern pink shrimp offer a sweet flavor and soft texture. Northern pink cold water shrimp are tiny in size and ideal for salads, soups, stuffings and casseroles.

Farm-raised white shrimp have a sweet, mild taste with a soft texture. Brown shrimp are rich in flavor and firm in texture, they make an excellent addition to sauces. Imported from the Far East, black tiger shrimp are mild in taste and have a soft texture.

Excellent taste and versatility make shrimp a delicious appetizer or main course.

A chilled shellfish combo platter with shrimp,
crab and oysters is the perfect appetizer at
City Crab Restaurant *in Manhattan.*

Shrimp Scampi

2 lbs. raw peeled jumbo shrimp
2 cloves finely chopped garlic
1 stick butter
Juice from 1 fresh lemon
1/4 cup olive oil
1 tablespoon dried parsley
3 tablespoons white wine
2 cups white rice

Cook rice according to package directions. Set aside and keep warm. Rinse shrimp with cold water and let drain in colander. In a skillet, melt butter and olive oil. Add garlic and saute several minutes until soft. Stir in lemon juice, parsley, white wine and shrimp.

Saute and baste shrimp 5-8 minutes until they turn pink and lose their glassy shine. Place rice on serving dish. Serve shrimp scampi with rice.

Serves 4

Smoked Salmon

Smoked salmon is produced primarily in the United States, Canada, Norway, Scotland and Ireland. Smoked salmon is processed by a hot or cold method. Cold smoked salmon has a moist, velvety texture. Hot smoked salmon has a firm, moist and flaky texture. The hot smoked process involves cooking salmon over high heat for a short time. Cold smoking methods are more similar to marination and take longer to produce.

A "brine" solution is the first step to producing smoked salmon. This process, which takes several days, cures the salmon. The brine solution is comprised of various spices, herbs and marinades which include salt, sugar, syrup, honey and liquor. After brining, wood from fruit trees, such as mesquite, hickory and cherry is used to smoke the salmon.

Lox is a brine cured salmon that has been lightly smoked. Nova refers to salmon that has been mildly cured and cold smoked. Its tradition originates from Nova Scotia, Canada.

Try cold smoked salmon on a fresh bagel with sliced ripe tomato, bermuda onion and a touch of cream cheese.

Smart Tips

● Smoked salmon should appear moist with a bright reddish-orange color.

● For optimum flavor and texture, remove smoked salmon from the refrigerator 20 minutes before serving.

● Gravlax is salmon that is cured for several days in fresh dill, salt, pepper and sugar.

● Cold smoked salmon is available pre-sliced for your convenience.

Smoked Salmon with Bowties

1 lb. bowtie pasta
1 stick butter
1/2 cup half & half
1/2 cup marinara sauce
8 oz. minced smoked salmon
1/4 teaspoon black pepper

Cook pasta until "al dente". Melt butter in a skillet. Slowly stir in half & half and marinara sauce. Let simmer on low heat for several minutes.

Add smoked salmon, and season to taste with black pepper. Place pasta in serving dish. Pour smoked salmon sauce over pasta.

Serves 4

Culinary Tip

●   For best results use a lightly salted smoked salmon in bowtie recipe.

Striped Bass

Striped bass is a culinary favorite throughout the world because of its great taste and year round availability. Farmed striped bass are mild in flavor and have a soft, flaky texture. In the United States, fresh water striped bass are farm-raised in Alabama, California, Florida, Mississippi and North Carolina.

Photo courtesy of Nature's Catch

After harvesting, farmed bass is packaged, loaded on trucks and distributed throughout the United States.

Wild striped bass are found along the Atlantic coast. These saltwater fish have a rich, sweet flavor and are tasty grilled or sauted.

*Atlantic striped bass is popular with
sport and commercial fishermen.*

Smart Tip

● Farmed striped bass range in size from 1 to 2.5 lbs. Small striped bass are ideal for baking or grilling. Striped bass that weigh over 2 lbs. are best when filleted.

Photo courtesy of Nature's Catch

Farmed bass are raised in pristine fresh water. Their grain-based diet ensures a delicious mild and sweet flavor.

Grilled Striped Bass

4 (1 1/4 lb.) whole striped bass
16 oz. Italian oil-based salad dressing

Rinse striped bass under cold tap water and let drain.
Baste fish thoroughly with dressing. Brush grate with oil.
Preheat grill on medium to high heat.

Place fish on grill. Cook on closed grill approximately
15-20 minutes or until meat begins to separate from bone.
Test with fork or knife. Avoid turning. Carefully remove from
grill with spatula.

Serves 4

Accompaniments:
grilled zucchini
grilled portobello mushrooms

Smart Tip

● Ask your seafood market to gut and remove scales from
whole striped bass to make preparation easier.

Sauted Striped Bass

2 lbs striped bass fillets
1 cup flour
1/2 teaspoon black pepper
1 stick butter
2 tablespoons olive oil
2 finely chopped cloves garlic
Juice from 1 fresh lemon
1/2 cup sliced fresh mushrooms
2 tablespoons white wine

Rinse striped bass fillets under cold water and drain. In a shallow dish, cover fillets with flour seasoned with black pepper. In a skillet combine butter, olive oil, garlic and let simmer for several minutes on low to medium heat until garlic softens. Add lemon juice, white wine, mushrooms and let simmer an additional two minutes on medium heat.

Place fillets in skillet. Cook 4-5 minutes on each side or until fish flakes easily with a fork. Carefully remove fillets from skillet with a spatula.

Serves 4

Accompaniments:
spinach
roasted potatoes

Squid (Calamari)

Caught in the Atlantic and Pacific Oceans, the loligo and illex are two popular types of squid consumed in America. Squid is imported from India, Europe, New Zealand, and Asia.

An excellent source of calcium and iron, squid has a mild flavor and tender texture. Cooking squid is considered an art by chefs in Mediterranean countries such as Greece, Italy and Spain. The most popular cooking methods for squid include boiling, sauteing and frying.

Serving fried calamari with marinara sauce is recommended.

Fried Squid (Calamari)

2 lbs. cleaned squid, cut into rings
1 1/2 cups vegetable oil
3 tablespoons water
1/2 teaspoon garlic powder
1 cup extra fine cracker meal
1 cup flour
4 eggs
1/2 teaspoon black pepper
2 tablespoons parmesan cheese
1/4 cup milk

Rinse squid rings and let drain in colander. In a separate bowl, combine eggs, milk, water and mix thoroughly. In a shallow dish, combine cracker meal, parmesan cheese and garlic powder. Set aside.

In a separate dish, place flour seasoned with black pepper. Coat squid with seasoned flour. Dip into egg mixture. Cover squid with cracker meal mixture.

Preheat vegetable oil in a large frying pan. Place squid into frying pan and cook 1-2 minutes until golden brown. Serve with warm marinara sauce or fresh lemon.

Serves 4

Whole Stuffed Calamari

2 lbs. cleaned squid tubes
2 tablespoons chopped onion
3 tablespoons olive oil
2 cups Italian bread crumbs
2 eggs
2 tablespoons parmesan cheese
2 (26 oz.) jars marinara sauce
1 lb. linguine
1/4 cup red wine

To prepare stuffing, heat olive oil in a large skillet. Saute onion on low heat for several minutes until soft. Add bread crumbs, eggs, parmesan cheese and mix well. Remove from stove.

Place stuffing inside of squid tubes. Use toothpicks to hold together. Heat marinara sauce in large skillet and let simmer on stove. Place whole stuffed squid into tomato sauce and cook 15 minutes. Add red wine. Prepare linguine "al dente" and serve.

Serves 4-6

Accompaniment:
escarole (See page 118.)

Surimi

Surimi is a processed combination of fish, egg whites, starches, sugars, flavors and other ingredients.

Several varieties of surimi include scallop, shrimp, lobster and crab. Crab is the most popular. Fully cooked and delicious in taste, surimi is a perfect addition to stuffings, pastas, casseroles and salads.

Smart Tip

● Carefully read the ingredient label on surimi. Less expensive brands of surimi list water as the first ingredient.

Surimi is produced from Alaskan pollock, or whiting. The fish is processed and then frozen into blocks.

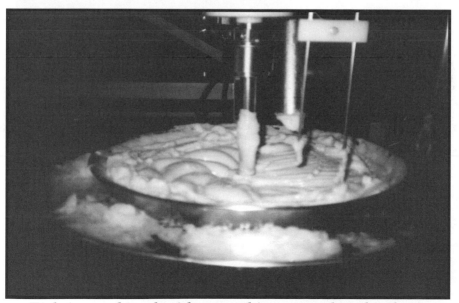

Fish is combined with egg whites, starches, binders, and other seafood extracts to produce surimi.

Seafood & Pasta Salad

1/2 lb. elbow macaroni
8 ozs. finely chopped imitation crab meat
1 cup mayonnaise
1/2 tsp. black pepper
1/2 cup white vinegar
3 tablespoons sugar
1/2 teaspoon vegetable oil
4 tablespoons lemon juice
2 tablespoons dried parsley

Prepare macaroni "al dente". Drain and let cool. Finely chop imitation crab meat and combine with macaroni in a large bowl.

In separate bowl, combine mayonnaise, black pepper, white vinegar, sugar, vegetable oil, lemon juice and parsley. Mix well. Combine mixture with pasta and crab meat. Toss gently and place in serving dish.

Serves 4-6

Swordfish

Swordfish is caught in warm waters around the world, and range in weight from 40 to over 500 lbs.

Rich in omega-3 oils, swordfish is well known for its distinctive flavor and firm texture. Swordfish is exceptional broiled, baked, pan seared or grilled.

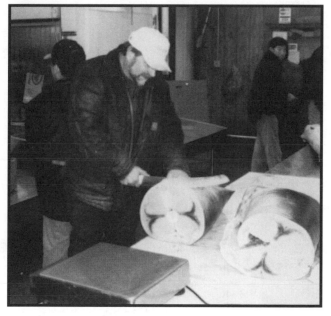

Fresh swordfish sliced to order at the Fulton Fish Market.

Smart Tip

● Fresh swordfish should appear moist and whitish pink in color.

● For milder taste, trim off dark line on swordfish steak before cooking.

Grilled Swordfish Kebabs

2 lbs. swordfish steaks
1 dozen cherry tomatoes
1 red bell pepper
1 yellow bell pepper
3 red skinned potatoes
1 large bermuda onion
8 whole fresh mushrooms
1/2 cup Italian oil-based salad dressing

Rinse swordfish under cold water. Cut and cube swordfish into 1 1/2 inch chunks. Slice peppers and onions into 1 1/2 inch pieces. Cook potatoes until slightly softened. Slice into 1 1/2 inch chunks.

On a skewer, alternate swordfish, peppers, potatoes, tomatoes, onions and mushrooms. Baste kebabs with salad dressing. Brush grate with oil. Preheat grill on medium to high heat. Place kebabs on grill and cook approximately 8-10 minutes on each side or until swordfish flakes easily with a fork. Continue to baste kebabs while cooking.

Serves 4

Tilapia

Photo courtesy of Rain Forest Aquaculture

*The pristine waters of Costa Rica
are home to farm-raised tilapia.*

Farm-raised in Costa Rica, Ecuador, Taiwan and the United States, fresh water tilapia reach their market size of 1 1/2 to 2 lbs. in approximately 18 months.

Well known for its lean white meat and mild flavor, tilapia is high in protein, low in fat, and contains omega-3 oils. Available as boneless fillets or whole fish, tilapia is delicious broiled, sauted or fried.

Smart Tip

● Fresh tilapia fillets should appear moist and whitish pink in color.

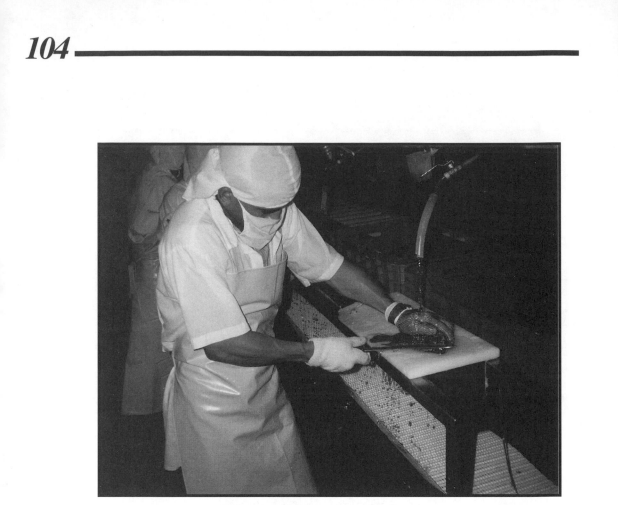

*Tilapia fillets prepared at a
farm in Canas, Costa Rica.*

Culinary Tip

- Tilapia is a delicious substitute for flounder, red snapper or orange roughy.

Tilapia Cutlets

*2 lbs. tilapia fillets
4 eggs
1/4 cup milk
1 cup flour
1/2 teaspoon black pepper
1/4 cup parmesan cheese
1 cup Italian seasoned bread crumbs
1 cup vegetable oil*

Rinse tilapia fillets and let drain. Mix eggs and milk together in a mixing bowl.

Dip tilapia fillets into flour seasoned with black pepper. Transfer fillets to egg mixture. In a separate dish, combine seasoned bread crumbs and parmesan cheese. Cover fillets completely with bread crumb mixture.

Heat vegetable oil in skillet. Fry approximately 1-2 minutes on each side or until golden brown. Serve with lemon wedges.

Serves 4

Accompaniments:
french fries
cole slaw

Tuna

Tuna's exotic appeal has been evident around the world for decades. Canned tuna is highly regarded as one of the foremost components of the American diet. Tuna is caught primarily along the east and west coasts of the United States, Hawaii, Ecuador and Venezuela.

The most popular varieties of tuna include albacore, bigeye, bluefin and yellowfin. The price of tuna is determined by its size, texture, fat content and color. Rich in flavor, tuna is high in protein, vitamins and minerals. Tuna tastes delicious grilled, baked or pan seared.

*Fresh yellowfin tuna on display
at the Fulton Fish Market.*

Smart Tips

● Fresh tuna should appear moist and red in color. Fresh albacore should appear pinkish white in color.

● Freshly cut tuna should be covered with plastic wrap to prevent from drying out and losing its natural color.

● Tombo refers to pink albacore tuna caught in the south Pacific. Ahi is a Hawaiian name for yellowfin or bigeye.

● Previously frozen tuna offers exceptional quality and taste.

Culinary Tips

● For a milder taste, trim off dark line on tuna steak before cooking.

● For optimum flavor, tuna should be served juicy. Avoid overcooking.

Pan Seared Tuna

2 lbs. tuna steaks
2 tablespoons olive oil
Juice from 1 fresh lemon
Black pepper to taste
1/2 teaspoon fresh chopped parsley

Rinse tuna under cold tap water and let drain. Preheat skillet. Baste tuna with olive oil and lemon juice. Sprinkle lightly with black pepper. Place steaks in hot skillet. Cook 3-4 minutes on each side or until fish flakes easily with fork. Garnish with parsley.

Serves 4

Accompaniments:
broccoli
white rice

Specialty Seafood Dishes

Lobster, Endive & Arugula Salad

8 oz. chopped lobster meat
1 bunch fresh arugula, rinsed and trimmed
1 fresh endive
1 stalk fresh anise (fennel)
2 oz. balsamic vinegar
4 oz. olive oil
1/4 teaspoon dried oregano
1/4 teaspoon black pepper
Shaved parmesan cheese to taste

Rinse arugula, endive and anise. Place arugula, endive, anise and lobster meat into a large salad bowl. In a separate container or bowl, mix balsamic vinegar, olive oil, black pepper and oregano. Pour dressing over salad and toss. Top with shaved parmesan cheese.

Serves 4

Spaghetti with Clams

3 dozen little neck clams
1 (26 oz.) jar marinara sauce
1 lb. spaghetti
Crushed red pepper to taste
Fresh parsley

Place clams in a large covered pot with two inches of water. Steam for approximately 12 minutes on high heat or until clams open. Discard any clams that do not open.

Cook spaghetti, and place on serving dish. In a saucepan, simmer marinara sauce on low heat. Pour marinara sauce and fresh clams over spaghetti. Lightly sprinkle with crushed red pepper. Garnish with fresh parsley.

Serves 4

Accompaniments:
garden salad
garlic bread

Seafood Cioppino

1/2 lb. cooked mussel meat
1/2 lb. bay or calico scallops
1/2 lb. raw peeled small or medium shrimp
1 lb. linguine
1/4 cup olive oil
2 cloves finely chopped garlic
1/2 cup minced onion
1 (28 oz.) can crushed tomatoes
8 oz. chicken broth
1 teaspoon oregano
1/4 teaspoon black pepper
1 bay leaf
2 tablespoons fresh parsley

In a large skillet, heat olive oil. Add onions and garlic. Saute several minutes until soft. Add tomatoes, chicken broth, oregano, black pepper and bay leaf to stock. Cook on low to medium heat for approximately 30 minutes. Stir often.

Add mussels, scallops and shrimp to skillet. Cook an additional 10 -12 minutes, stirring frequently. Remove bay leaf. Cook linguine and place on serving dish. Pour seafood cioppino over pasta. Garnish with fresh parsley.

Serves 4

Shrimp Risotto

2 lbs. raw peeled medium or large shrimp
1/4 cup chopped red bell peppers
2 tablespoons olive oil
1 clove finely chopped garlic
1/2 cup chopped onion
1 1/2 cups risotto
1/4 cup peas
1/2 stick butter

Combine oil, butter, onion, garlic and peppers in a skillet and saute several minutes until soft. Add shrimp and cook for approximately 5 minutes on each side or until shrimp turn pink. Add peas.

Simmer an additional two minutes. Set aside and keep warm. In a separate skillet, prepare risotto according to package directions. Place risotto on serving dish and pour shrimp over risotto.

Serves 4

Shrimp Fra Diavolo

1 1/2 lbs. raw peeled medium or large shrimp
1 (26 oz.) jar marinara sauce
1 lb. angel hair pasta
Crushed red pepper to taste
2 cloves finely chopped garlic
1 teaspoon dried parsley
1 tablespoon olive oil
2 tablespoons butter

Rinse shrimp and let drain in a colander. In a skillet, combine butter, olive oil and garlic. Saute garlic on low heat for several minutes until soft. Add shrimp and cook uncovered for approximately 5 minutes on each side, until shrimp turn pink. Remove from heat.

In a separate saucepan, heat marinara sauce and season to taste with crushed red pepper. Remove shrimp from skillet, add to marinara sauce. Cook pasta and place in serving dish. Top with shrimp and marinara sauce.

Serves 4

Accompaniments:
garlic bread
arugula, endive and radicchio salad

Swordfish Balsamico

2 lbs. swordfish steaks
1/2 cup balsamic vinegar
1/3 cup chicken broth
3/4 cup fresh mushrooms
1 cup flour
1/2 teaspoon garlic powder
1/2 teaspoon paprika
3 tablespoons olive oil
Salt and pepper to taste

Rinse swordfish under cold tap water and let drain. In a separate shallow bowl, cover swordfish in flour seasoned with salt and pepper.

Preheat oil in skillet on medium heat and add swordfish. Add balsamic vinegar, chicken broth and mushrooms. Sprinkle with paprika and garlic powder. Cook 3-4 minutes on each side or until swordfish flakes easily with a fork. Do not overcook. Swordfish should be served slightly juicy.

Serves 4

Accompaniments:
white rice
string beans

Lobster & Broccoli Rabe with Rigatoni

1/2 lb. cooked lobster meat
1 bunch broccoli rabe
1 lb. rigatoni
1 tablespoon butter
3 tablespoons olive oil
1 chopped ripe tomato
1/2 teaspoon dried basil, oregano and garlic powder
Salt and black pepper to taste

Trim and rinse broccoli rabe. Heat olive oil and butter on low heat in a large skillet. Add broccoli rabe and tomato. Season with garlic powder, oregano, basil, salt and pepper. Saute approximately 15 minutes until tender.

Add lobster meat and let simmer an additional 2 minutes. Prepare pasta "al dente", and place in serving dish. Top with lobster and broccoli rabe.

Serves 4

Accompaniment:
Italian bread

White Clam Sauce with Linguine

1 lb. linguine
3 (6.5 oz.) cans cooked chopped clams with broth
1/2 cup butter
1/4 cup olive oil
2 tablespoons finely chopped parsley
1/2 teaspoon dried basil
1/4 teaspoon black pepper
2 cloves finely chopped garlic

In a skillet, preheat butter and oil on low heat. Add garlic and saute for several minutes until soft. Stir in basil, pepper, parsley and clams. Let simmer approximately 4 minutes.

Prepare linguine and place in serving dish. Pour clam sauce over linguine.

Serves 4

Accompaniments:
mesclun salad
Italian bread

Sauted Escarole

1 1/2 lbs. escarole
4 tablespoons butter
1/4 cup olive oil
2 cloves of finely chopped garlic
1 tablespoon finely chopped onion
Salt and black pepper to taste

Rinse escarole and separate into 4 inch pieces. Steam escarole 2 to 3 minutes until tender.

In a saucepan melt oil and butter on low heat. Saute garlic and onions until soft. Add escarole and continue to saute for an additional 3 to 4 minutes. Season to taste with salt and black pepper.

Serves 4

Traditional Seafood Fare

Crab Cakes

1 lb. lump crab meat
1 egg
1 stick butter
2 tablespoons lemon juice
2 tablespoons dried parsley
3/4 cup bread crumbs
1/4 teaspoon black pepper
1 cup extra fine cracker meal
1 cup vegetable oil

In a mixing bowl, combine melted butter with egg, lemon juice, parsley and black pepper. Mix well.

In a separate bowl, combine bread crumbs with crab meat. Add egg mixture to crab meat. Gently mix all ingredients together. Form into cakes about 1 inch thick.

Coat with cracker meal. Preheat vegetable oil in a frying pan and deep fry until golden brown.

Serves 4

Grilled Shrimp with Arugula

1 lb. raw peeled jumbo shrimp
1 cup balsamic vinaigrette
2 bunches fresh arugula
Shaved parmesan cheese to taste
Black pepper to taste

Rinse shrimp under cold tap water and let drain in colander.
Baste shrimp with vinaigrette. Brush grate with oil. Preheat
grill on medium to high heat. Grill shrimp for 6-8 minutes or
until shrimp turn pink and lose their glassy shine.
Do not overcook.

Cut and rinse arugula. Place arugula in the center of serving
dish. Arrange shrimp around the perimeter of the plate.
Pour remaining vinaigrette over shrimp and arugula. Top
with black pepper and shaved parmesan cheese.

Serves 4

Bob & Joe's Clambake

6 live (1 1/2 lb.) lobsters
6 dozen cherrystone or littleneck clams
6 red skinned potatoes
6 ears of corn
1/4 cup white vinegar
1 quart water

On stove or outdoor grill, place water and vinegar into large pot. Boil water and place lobsters in pot. Cover pot. Cook lobsters approximately 12 minutes. Remove lobsters when they turn bright red. Cool for 15 minutes.

Wrap each husked ear of corn and each potato in foil and place on outdoor grill.

Place clams individually on outdoor grill. Close grill. Check periodically and remove clams from grill as they open. Discard any clams that do not open.

Serve with melted butter and lemon.

Serves 6

Accompaniments:
cole slaw (See page 171.)
potato salad (See page 172.)

Grilled Rainbow Trout

2 lbs. rainbow trout fillets
2 tablespoons olive oil
2 tablespoons lemon juice
2 teaspoons minced garlic
1/2 teaspoon black pepper
1/4 cup finely chopped scallions

Rinse two pounds of rainbow trout fillets under cold tap water. In a bowl mix olive oil, lemon juice, garlic, black pepper and chopped scallions. Cover fillets generously with marinade.

Before preheating grill on medium to high heat, brush grate with oil. Place trout fillets skin side down. Baste often. Grill 6 minutes on each side or until fish flakes easily with a fork.

Serves 4

Accompaniments:
grilled red skinned potatoes
grilled sliced eggplant

Grilled Tuna Caesar

1 lb. tuna steaks
1 (8 oz.) jar Caesar salad dressing
1 head romaine lettuce
2 ripe tomatoes
1 small bermuda onion
2 tablespoons olive oil
1/4 teaspoon black pepper

Rinse tuna under cold tap water and let drain. Baste tuna with olive oil and pepper. Brush grate with oil. Preheat grill on medium to high heat.

Grill tuna 5-6 minutes on each side or until tuna flakes easily with a fork. Do not overcook. While grilling, baste tuna frequently with marinade. Remove from grill and let cool.

Arrange lettuce, onions and tomatoes on serving dish. Top with flaked grilled tuna and Caesar dressing.

Serves 4

Spicy Shrimp & Mushrooms

2 lbs. raw peeled medium or large shrimp
1 1/2 sticks butter
1 1/2 tablespoons olive oil
1/2 lb. sliced fresh mushrooms
1/4 cup chicken broth
1/4 cup chopped scallions
1/2 teaspoon each of cayenne pepper,
   black pepper, white pepper, garlic powder,
   oregano, thyme, basil and salt
2 tablespoons dried parsley

Rinse shrimp under cold tap water and let drain. Combine spices with butter and olive oil, melt on low heat in large skillet. Add shrimp and saute several minutes on medium heat. Stir in mushrooms and chicken broth. Saute 2 additional minutes until shrimp turn pink.

Serves 4

Accompaniments:
wild rice
Italian bread

Clams Oreganata

2 dozen littleneck or topneck clams
3/4 cup Italian seasoned bread crumbs
2 tablespoons parmesan cheese
1/4 teaspoon garlic powder
1/3 cup olive oil

Rinse and open live clams. Loosen clam meat from bottom shell. Place clams on the half shell in a shallow baking pan.

In a mixing bowl, combine bread crumbs, parmesan cheese, garlic powder and olive oil. Mix well to create a paste. Spread bread crumb mixture evenly over clams. Broil 6-8 minutes or until lightly brown. Serve with fresh lemon wedges.

Serves 4

Culinary Tip

● To open easily, wrap clams in damp paper towel and microwave on high power for approximately 1 minute.

Shrimp Bruschetta

8 oz. *cooked tiny or small shrimp*
4 ripe tomatoes, diced
4 tablespoons balsamic vinegar
1/2 cup olive oil
1 tablespoon lemon juice
1/4 teaspoon garlic powder
1/4 teaspoon black pepper
2 tablespoons fresh chopped basil
1 loaf baguette or Italian bread

Rinse shrimp and let drain in colander. In a mixing bowl, combine tomatoes, olive oil, balsamic vinegar, garlic powder, black pepper, basil, and lemon juice. Mix well.

Slice bread, brush with olive oil and toast lightly. Spoon mixture on top of toasted bread.

Serves 4-6

Distinctive
Seafood Meals

Crawfish Creole

1 lb. cooked crawfish tail meat
2 cups marinara sauce
1/4 cup butter
2 tablespoons olive oil
1 cup chicken broth
1/4 cup diced red bell peppers
1/4 cup diced green bell peppers
1/2 cup finely chopped onions
1 teaspoon finely chopped garlic
4 cups cooked white rice
1/2 teaspoon each of black pepper, cayenne pepper,
   white pepper, dried basil and oregano

Prepare rice according to package directions. Set aside
and keep warm. In a large skillet, melt butter and oil. Add
onions, peppers and garlic, saute until soft. Add chicken
broth, marinara sauce and seasonings. Simmer on low heat
for approximately 10 minutes, stirring frequently. Add
crawfish and simmer several additional minutes. Place rice
on serving dish. Pour creole sauce over rice.

Serves 4

Accompaniments:
French bread
spinach salad

Elegant Seafood Dinner for Four

*A fresh bouquet of flowers, candlelight and fine dinnerware
set the mood for an elegant seafood dinner.*

Shrimp Cocktail
Stuffed Mushrooms with Crabmeat
Lobster with Angel Hair Pasta

Shrimp Cocktail

Arrange approximately 24 cooked jumbo shrimp on serving dish. Serve chilled with fresh lemon wedges and cocktail sauce.

Stuffed Mushrooms with Crabmeat

16 large mushrooms
12 oz. backfin crab meat
2 tablespoon olive oil
1/4 cup finely chopped celery
3/4 cup finely chopped onion
2 cloves finely chopped garlic
1 tablespoon dried basil
1/4 cup chopped parsley
1/2 cup bread crumbs
Salt and black pepper to taste

Rinse mushrooms and remove stems. Preheat oil in skillet on medium heat. Add onions, celery and garlic and saute until tender. Add basil, parsley, bread crumbs, salt, black pepper and crab meat. Saute several additional minutes. Remove from heat and let cool.

Stuff crab meat mixture into mushroom caps. Place in 350 degree preheated oven and bake approximately 10 minutes until golden brown. Serve with fresh lemon.

Lobster with Angel Hair Pasta

12 oz. cooked lobster meat
1 lb. angel hair pasta
1 stick butter
1/2 cup olive oil
3 tablespoons white wine
1/2 teaspoon black pepper
2 cloves finely chopped garlic
3 tablespoons parsley

Melt butter and olive oil in skillet on low heat. Add garlic and saute until soft. Add black pepper, parsley and lobster meat and bring to a simmer. Add white wine. Let simmer two additional minutes.

Cook pasta, place on serving dish. Top with lobster sauce.

Accompaniments:
mesclun salad with balsamic vinaigrette
escarole (See page 118.)
cheese cake

Broiled Tilapia Parmesan

2 lbs. tilapia fillets
1 tablespoon olive oil
1/2 stick butter
1/4 cup Italian bread crumbs
2 tablespoons parmesan cheese
Juice from 2 fresh lemons

Rinse tilapia under cold water and let drain. Spread olive oil on the bottom of a broiling pan. Place fillets on broiling pan.

In a bowl mix parmesan cheese with bread crumbs. Lightly sprinkle bread crumb mixture on fillets. Melt butter, add lemon juice and pour over fillets. Broil approximately 10 minutes or until fillets flake easily with a fork.

Serves 4

Accompaniments:
string beans
roasted potatoes

Lemon Buttered Salmon

2 lbs. boneless salmon fillets
1 stick butter
1 tablespoon fresh chopped parsley
1 tablespoon fresh chopped basil
1/4 teaspoon black pepper
Juice from 1 fresh lemon

Rinse salmon under cold tap water and let drain. Melt butter.
Add lemon juice, parsley, basil, pepper, and mix well.
Preheat oven to 350 degrees. Cover baking pan with foil.
Dip fillets in seasoned butter sauce and place on baking
pan. Pour remainder of sauce over fillets and bake 15 to 20
minutes or until fish flakes easily with a fork.

Serves 4

Accompaniments:
asparagus
wild rice

Culinary Tip

● Alternative: Lemon buttered salmon tastes delicious
prepared on the grill. Place buttered fillets on foil and grill
on medium to high heat approximately 20-25 minutes or until
salmon flakes easily with a fork.

Shrimp with Linguine

1 lb. raw peeled medium or large shrimp
1 lb. linguine
1 (26 oz.) jar marinara sauce
3 tablespoons chopped fresh basil
1/4 teaspoon garlic powder
Black pepper to taste
2 tablespoons olive oil

Rinse shrimp under cold tap water and let drain. In a large saucepan, combine marinara sauce, basil, garlic powder and black pepper. Let simmer approximately 10 minutes on low heat.

Heat olive oil in a separate skillet on low to medium heat, add shrimp. Saute shrimp, stirring frequently, until shrimp turn pink and lose their glassy shine. Remove shrimp individually and add to marinara sauce. Cook linguine "al dente" and place on serving dish. Pour shrimp marinara over linguine.

Serves 4

Accompaniments:
garden salad
garlic bread

Pan Fried Catfish

2 lbs. catfish fillets
3/4 cup yellow cornmeal
1/4 cup flour
3/4 teaspoon cayenne pepper
1/4 teaspoon each of black pepper, salt, dried parsley
1 cup vegetable oil

Rinse catfish under cold water and let drain. Combine corn meal, flour, cayenne, black pepper, parsley and salt in a bowl.

Preheat oil in a large skillet on high heat. Place fillets in skillet and cook 2-3 minutes on each side or until fillets are lightly brown and flake easily with a fork.

Serves 4

Accompaniments:
oven fried chips (See page 163.)
macaroni salad (See page 173.)

Seafood Stir Fry

1/2 lb. bay or calico scallops
1/2 lb. raw peeled medium or large shrimp
2 cups white rice
1 (14 oz.) package frozen stir fry vegetables
1 (14 oz.) jar oriental stir fry sauce
3 tablespoons vegetable oil

Prepare rice according to package directions. Set aside and keep warm. Rinse vegetables and place in preheated wok or large frying pan with oil. Saute vegetables 4-6 minutes until tender. Add stir fry sauce, scallops and shrimp. Continue cooking an additional 4-6 minutes until shrimp and scallops lose their glassy shine. Place rice on serving dish and top with seafood stir fry.

Serves 4

Shrimp Tempura

2 lbs. raw peeled jumbo or collossal shrimp
1 cup flour
2 eggs
1/4 cup milk
3/4 cup vegetable oil
Salt and pepper to taste

Rinse shrimp with cold tap water and drain in colander. In a bowl mix eggs and milk together. Cover shrimp with flour that has been seasoned to taste with salt and pepper. Dip shrimp in batter. Heat oil in large skillet. Fry until golden brown.

Serves 4

Accompaniments:
white rice
string beans

Shrimp Fried Rice

1 lb. raw peeled small or medium shrimp
2 tablespoons sliced scallion
1 teaspoon chopped garlic
3 tablespoons chopped onion
1 egg, slightly beaten
1 1/2 cups long grained rice
1/4 cup frozen peas
1/2 cup fresh mushrooms
1 1/2 tablespoons vegetable oil
2 tablespoons butter

Cook rice according to package directions. Set aside and keep warm. Heat oil and butter on low heat in a skillet. Add garlic and onions, saute until soft. Add egg and stir for approximately 15 seconds.

Add shrimp, peas and mushrooms to egg mixture. Saute on medium heat for several minutes until shrimp turn pink and lose their glassy shine. Add rice and scallions. Saute 2 additional minutes.

Serves 4

Scrumptious Seafood Dishes for Kids

Fried Tilapia Fingers

2 lbs. tilapia fillets
4 eggs
1/4 cup milk
1 cup flour
Black pepper to taste
3/4 cup vegetable oil
1/4 cup parmesan cheese
1 cup Italian seasoned bread crumbs

Rinse tilapia fillets under cold tap water. Cut tilapia fillets into approximately two inch strips. In a bowl mix eggs and milk together. Cover tilapia in flour that has been seasoned to taste with black pepper.Dip tilapia into egg mixture. In a separate bowl, mix seasoned bread crumbs and parmesan cheese. Cover tilapia completely with bread crumb mixture.

Preheat vegetable oil in a frying pan and fry tilapia approximately 1-2 minutes until golden brown.

Serve with sweet and sour sauce or ketchup.

Serves 4

Accompaniments:
french fries
cole slaw

Codfish Cakes

2 lbs. cooked cod fillet
2 cups cold mashed potatoes
2 eggs
2 tablespoons butter
2 tablespoons dried parsley
1/4 teaspoon white pepper
1/4 teaspoon garlic powder
1 cup extra fine cracker meal
1 cup vegetable oil

Bake or saute cod and let cool in refrigerator. Prepare mashed potatoes and let cool. Melt butter. In a large bowl, combine cod, mashed potatoes, eggs, butter, parsley, pepper and garlic powder. Mix well.

Form into cakes about one inch thick. Coat with cracker meal. Preheat vegetable oil in a large frying pan and fry approximately 2 minutes until golden brown.

Serves 4

Shrimp Fajitas

2 lbs. raw peeled small or medium shrimp
3 teaspoons olive oil
1 clove finely chopped garlic
1 red bell pepper
1 green bell pepper
1 yellow bell pepper
2 medium onions
3 tablespoons lemon juice
3 tablespoons water
1/2 teaspoon chili powder
10 flour tortillas

Slice peppers and onions into thin strips. Heat oil in large skillet on medium heat. Add garlic, peppers, and onions. Saute until soft.

In a bowl, combine shrimp, lemon juice, water and chili powder. Mix well. Pour shrimp and marinade into skillet. Cook several minutes until shrimp turn pink and lose their glassy shine. Place on serving dish and serve with warm tortillas.

Serves 6-8

Seafood Tacos

4 taco shells
1 lb. finely chopped imitation crab meat
2 cups shredded lettuce
2 cups diced tomatoes
8 oz. shredded cheddar cheese
1 (1.25 oz.) packet taco seasoning mix
2 (5 oz.) jars taco sauce

In a saucepan, combine imitation crab meat, taco mix and 5 oz. taco sauce, heat for several minutes.

Fill taco shells with crab meat mixture. Spoon in lettuce, tomatoes, cheddar cheese and taco sauce to taste.

Serves 4

Macaroni & Cheese with Crab

1 lb. elbow macaroni
8 oz. shredded cheddar cheese
4 oz. imitation crab meat
3 tablespoons butter

Cook pasta "al dente". Place pasta in casserole dish.
Melt butter and pour over pasta. Set aside and keep warm.

Finely chop crab meat, mix with pasta. Top with cheddar
cheese. Heat in oven or microwave until cheese melts.

Serves 4

Shrimp Focaccia

2 (12.5 oz.) focaccia bread
2 cups shredded mozzarella cheese
1 (16 oz.) jar of marinara sauce
1 lb. cooked tiny or small shrimp
4 teaspoons parmesan cheese
2 tablespoons olive oil

Preheat oven to 375 degrees. Brush focaccia with olive oil.
Spread marinara sauce evenly over focaccia. Sprinkle
mozzarella cheese on top.

Bake approximately 8-10 minutes. Remove from oven.
Spread shrimp and parmesan cheese evenly over focaccia.
Bake an additional 3 minutes or until crispy.

Serves 4

Seafood Quesadillas

1/2 lb. cooked tiny or small shrimp
2 cups shredded jalapeno jack or cheddar cheese
1/4 teaspoon crab seasoning
8 small flour tortillas
1/4 cup butter
1 cup salsa

In a bowl combine shrimp, cheese and crab seasoning. Spread mixture over 4 tortillas and cover with remaining tortillas.

Melt butter in skillet on low heat. With a spatula, carefully place quesadillas into skillet and cook approximately two minutes on each side. Allow to cool. Serve with salsa.

Serves 4

Culinary Tip

● Finely chopped imitation crab meat can be substituted for shrimp in quesadillas.

Shrimp Lasagne

1 lb. cooked small or medium shrimp
8 oz. oven ready lasagne
1 lb. ricotta cheese
1 egg, beaten
1 lb. shredded mozzarella cheese
1 (26 oz.) jar marinara sauce
1/2 teaspoon each of dried oregano, basil, black pepper
1/4 teaspoon each of salt and dried parsley

In a bowl, combine ricotta cheese, egg, basil, oregano, salt, parsley, and black pepper. Mix well and set aside.

In a lasagne pan, spread marinara sauce generously to cover bottom of pan. Place a single layer of lasagne over marinara sauce. Spread enough ricotta cheese mixture to cover lasagne. Sprinkle 1 cup of mozzarella cheese. Repeat to form two more layers.

Cover with foil and place in a preheated oven. Bake at 375 degrees for approximately 25 minutes. Remove from oven. Remove foil. Spread shrimp evenly over lasagne, then top with remaining mozzarella cheese. Place uncovered lasagne in oven and cook an additional 12-15 minutes until cheese is melted. Let cool for 10 minutes.

Serves 4

Soups, Sauces, Dips and More

New England Clam Chowder

3 cans (6.5 oz.) cooked chopped clams with broth
1 cup chicken broth
1 stick butter
2 cups peeled & diced potatoes
1/2 cup chopped onion
1 cup chopped celery
2 cups milk
1 cup light cream
1/2 teaspoon white pepper
1/4 teaspoon salt
5 tablespoons flour

In a large pot, combine celery, onions, butter and chicken broth. Cook celery and onions on medium heat for approximately 25 minutes until soft. Add potatoes to stock and cook for an additional 25 minutes.

In a bowl, combine milk and flour. Mix well. Slowly combine milk mixture with chowder, stir well. Add clam broth, light cream, white pepper and salt to mixture. Let simmer an additional 10-12 minutes on medium heat. Stir frequently.

Serves 6

Manhattan Clam Chowder

4 cans (6.5 oz.) cooked chopped clams with broth
2 cups chicken broth
1 cup chopped celery
1/2 cup chopped onion
2 1/2 cups peeled and diced potatoes
1 can (28 oz.) crushed tomatoes
1 cup marinara sauce
1 bay leaf
1/2 teaspoon each of black pepper, dried oregano,
    basil, sugar
1/4 teaspoon salt

In a large pot, combine celery, onions, butter, crushed tomatoes, chicken broth, tomatoes and spices. Cook celery and onions on medium heat for approximately 25 minutes until soft.

Add potatoes to stock and cook for an additional 25 minutes. Add clams with broth. Let simmer an additional 10 minutes. Remove bay leaf and serve.

Serves 8-10

Fish Chowder

1 lb. boneless halibut, cod or haddock fillets
1 1/2 cups chopped celery
1 cup onion
1/2 cup carrots
1 1/2 cups rice or pastina
1 large can (48 oz.) chicken broth
5 cups water
1 cup diced tomato
1 cup frozen peas
1/2 teaspoon each of basil, thyme,
   savory, black pepper and salt
3 tablespoons dried parsley

Slice fish into small 1 1/2 inch pieces. Rinse fish and drain. Set aside. Combine all ingredients except fish and peas in a large pot. Bring to a boil. Add fish and peas. Cover pot and simmer on low to medium heat for approximately 50 minutes. Stir frequently.

Serves 8-10

Shrimp Bisque

8 oz. cooked small shrimp
1 cup sliced mushrooms
1/2 cup finely chopped onion
1 stick butter
2 cans tomato soup
2 tablespoons flour
16 oz. milk
8 oz. light cream
1/2 cup dry cooking sherry

Melt butter in large pot. Add onion and saute approximately 5 minutes on low heat until soft. Add shrimp, mushrooms and simmer an additional 2 minutes on medium heat.

Add tomato soup and stir. In a separate bowl, combine milk, flour and light cream, slowly add to stock. Add sherry, stir and let simmer on low heat for approximately 8-10 minutes. Stir frequently.

Serves 6

Culinary Tip

● Bisque can be prepared using lobster as a substitute for shrimp.

Bouillabaisse

1/2 lb. boneless cod fillet
1/2 lb. calico or bay scallops
1/2 lb. raw peeled medium shrimp
1 large can (48 oz.) chicken broth
6 cups water
1 can (28 oz.) crushed tomatoes
2 cups chopped onions
3/4 cup chopped celery
3/4 cup chopped carrots
1/2 cup uncooked rice
3 tablespoons dried parsley
1/2 teaspoon each of dried thyme, basil, oregano,
  salt, garlic powder and black pepper
1/2 cup frozen peas

Cut cod into small 1 1/2 inch pieces. Rinse cod, shrimp and scallops under cold tap water and drain in colander.

Combine all ingredients except seafood and peas in a large pot. Bring to a boil. Add seafood and peas. Cook on low to medium heat for approximately 50 minutes, stirring often.

Serves 8-10

Culinary Tip

●   Sliced sea scallops may be substituted for calico or bay scallops in bouillabaisse.

Shrimp Pasta Fagioli

1/2 lb. raw peeled small or medium shrimp
1/2 lb. dry great northern beans
1 cup elbow macaroni
3 tablespoons olive oil
1/2 cup chopped onion
1/4 cup chopped celery
1/2 cup sliced carrots
1/2 cup sliced escarole
1 can (14 1/2 oz.) crushed tomatoes
1 cup chicken broth
1/2 teaspoon each of basil, oregano, garlic powder, salt
1/4 teaspoon black pepper
3 cups water

In a large covered pot, soak beans overnight in water. Retain water, do not drain.

Heat olive oil in a skillet. Add onion, celery and carrots, saute several minutes until softened. Add tomatoes, escarole and spices into stock. Simmer on low to medium heat for several minutes.

Combine vegetable mixture with beans. Add chicken broth, macaroni and shrimp. Cook approximately 10 minutes until pasta and beans are "al dente". Stir frequently.

Serves 6-8

Shrimp Nachos

1 lb. shredded cheddar or mozzarella cheese
8 oz. cooked tiny or small shrimp
1 ripe tomato, diced
1 bag nachos chips

Place nachos in casserole dish. Sprinkle cheese, shrimp and tomato evenly over nachos. Heat in oven or microwave until cheese melts.

Serve 4

Balsamic Marinade

1/2 cup olive oil
1/4 cup balsamic oil
3 tablespoons water
1/4 teaspoon each of garlic powder, black pepper
1/2 teaspoon each of oregano, basil
1 tablespoon lemon juice

Combine all ingredients in a bowl and mix thoroughly.
Before cooking seafood and vegetables, baste with
marinade. Continue to baste while cooking.

Oil and Lemon Marinade

3 tablespoons lemon juice
1/4 cup olive oil
1/4 teaspoon black pepper
1/2 teaspoon each of garlic powder, dried parsley, basil

Combine all ingredients in a mixing bowl. Before cooking seafood and vegetables, baste with marinade. Continue to baste while cooking.

Spicy Crab Dip

8 oz. backfin crab meat
8 oz. lite softened cream cheese
1/4 teaspoon cayenne pepper
1/4 teaspoon garlic powder
2 tablespoons milk
1 teaspoon chopped scallions
1/2 cup chopped tomatoes

Preheat oven to 350 degrees. In an oven-safe dish, combine crab meat, cream cheese, cayenne pepper, garlic powder, milk and tomatoes.

Bake for 20 minutes at 350 degrees. Garnish with scallions. Serve with raw vegetables or tortilla chips.

Seasoning for Broiled Seafood

1 cup extra fine cracker meal
1/3 cup grated parmesan cheese
1/2 teaspoon garlic powder
1 tablespoon dried parsley

In a bowl, combine all ingredients and mix well. Sprinkle mixture and melted butter on seafood before broiling.

Clam Salsa

1 (6 1/2 oz.) can of cooked chopped clams
1 (16 oz.) jar of salsa
1 bag nacho chips

Combine salsa with chopped clams and serve with nacho chips.

Oven Fried Chips

6 medium potatoes
1 stick butter
1/4 teaspoon crab seasoning
Salt to taste

Rinse potatoes. Preheat oven to 450 degrees. Slice potatoes approximately 1/8 to 1/4 inch thick.

Butter a large baking pan. Place potatoes in pan. Melt butter. Mix in crab seasoning. Pour evenly over potatoes. Bake for approximately 45 minutes or until crispy golden brown. Salt to taste.

Serves 6

Breading for Fried Seafood

1 cup seasoned Italian bread crumbs
1/3 cup parmesan cheese

In a bowl, combine ingredients and mix well.

Cocktail Sauce

1 cup ketchup
Juice from 1 fresh lemon
3 teaspoons white horseradish
1/2 teaspoon worcestershire sauce

Combine ketchup, lemon juice, horseradish and worcestershire sauce in a bowl. Mix well.

Tartar Sauce

1 cup mayonnaise
4 tablespoons chopped dill pickle
1 tablespoon finely chopped Spanish onion
Juice from 1/2 fresh lemon

Combine all ingredients in a bowl. Mix well. Refrigerate until
ready to use.

Marinara Sauce

1/4 cup olive oil
3/4 cup finely chopped onion
4 cloves finely chopped garlic
2 (1 lb.12 oz.) cans crushed tomatoes
1 tablespoon dried basil
1 tablespoon sugar
1 tablespoon salt
1/2 teaspoon black pepper
1/4 cup red wine

Heat olive oil in a large saucepan, add onion and garlic.
Saute on low heat until soft.

Add tomatoes, basil, sugar, black pepper and salt. Simmer
for approximately 45 minutes, stirring frequently. Add red
wine and simmer an additional 5 minutes.

Signature Salads

Cole Slaw

2 cups shredded green cabbage
1/2 cup shredded carrots
1/2 cup white vinegar
3 tablespoons sugar
Juice from 1/2 fresh lemon
1/2 teaspoon vegetable oil
1 1/2 cups mayonnaise
Salt to taste

In a large bowl, mix cabbage and carrots. In a separate bowl, mix vinegar, sugar, lemon juice, vegetable oil and mayonnaise.

Combine ingredients together. Mix well. Salt to taste.

Serves 6

Culinary Tip

● As a timesaver, purchase pre-shredded cole slaw.

Potato Salad

6 large potatoes
3/4 cup chopped celery
1/4 cup chopped onion
1/2 cup white vinegar
3 tablespoons sugar
Juice from 1/2 fresh lemon
1/2 teaspoon vegetable oil
1 cup mayonnaise
Salt to taste
1 1/2 tablespoons dried parsley

Cook potatoes until slightly softened. Rinse potatoes in colander with cold water, peel potatoes and refrigerate approximately 20 minutes.

Slice chilled potatoes into 1/2 inch thick pieces. Salt potatoes to taste. Place potatoes into large mixing bowl. Add celery, onions, and parsley. Gently mix.

In a separate bowl, mix vinegar, sugar, lemon juice, vegetable oil and mayonnaise. Add mixture to potatoes and mix gently.

Serves 6

Macaroni Salad

1/2 lb. elbow macaroni
1/2 cup shredded carrots
2 tablespoons dried parsley
1/2 cup white vinegar
3 tablespoons sugar
Juice from 1/2 fresh lemon
1/2 teaspoon vegetable oil
1 cup mayonnaise

Cook pasta "al dente". Place pasta in large mixing bowl.
Add carrots and mix well.

In a separate bowl, mix vinegar, sugar, parsley, lemon juice,
vegetable oil and mayonnaise. Add to pasta and mix
thoroughly. Salt to taste.

Serves 6

Tuna Salad

1 (12 oz.) can albacore tuna, in water
3/4 cup finely chopped celery
4 tablespoons finely chopped onion
4 tablespoons lemon juice
1/2 teaspoon salt
1/4 teaspoon black pepper
1/2 cup mayonnaise

In a bowl, combine tuna, celery and onions. Add lemon juice, salt, pepper and mayonnaise. Mix thoroughly.

Serve with fresh pita bread or on a bed of crisp romaine lettuce.

Serves 6

Culinary Tip

• Squeeze excess water from tuna, celery and onions.

Mediterranean Seafood Salad

12 oz. raw peeled medium shrimp
12 oz. cleaned squid, cut into rings
1/4 cup pitted and sliced olives
1/4 cup sliced roasted peppers, drained
1/4 cup olive oil
1/4 cup lemon juice
1/2 teaspoon garlic powder
1 teaspoon dried oregano
1 teaspoon dried basil
2 tablespoons dried parsley
1/4 teaspoon salt
1/4 teaspoon black pepper

In a medium pot, bring 1 1/2 quarts of water to a boil. Add shrimp and squid. Cook until shrimp and squid lose their glassy shine. Check frequently. Rinse in colander under cold tap water.

Place cooked shrimp and squid in a large bowl. Add roasted peppers and black olives. In a separate bowl, combine olive oil, lemon juice, parsley, oregano, salt and pepper. Combine marinade with shrimp and squid. Mix well.

Serves 6

Culinary Tip

● After boiling, immediately rinse squid and shrimp with cold tap water to slow down cooking process.

Shrimp Fusilli

1 lb. fusilli pasta
1/2 tablespoon olive oil
1/2 cup chopped ripe tomatoes
1 (8 oz.) can small pitted black olives
1 cup chopped red bell pepper
1/4 cup finely chopped onion
1 (8 oz.) jar Italian oil-based salad dressing
1/2 lb. cubed mozzarella cheese
1/2 lb. cooked medium or large shrimp
1 tablespoon freshly chopped parsley

Cook pasta "al dente". Place pasta into large mixing bowl.
Mix olive oil into pasta and let cool. Add tomatoes, parsley,
black olives, peppers, onions, mozzarella and shrimp.
Mix gently. Add salad dressing and refrigerate for 30
minutes before serving.

Serves 8

Shrimp with Roasted Peppers

3/4 lb. cooked medium or large shrimp
1 lb. sliced roasted peppers
2 cloves chopped garlic
1 teaspoon fresh chopped basil
1/2 teaspoon black pepper
1/3 cup olive oil
Juice from 1 fresh lemon

Rinse shrimp and let drain in colander. In a large mixing bowl, combine shrimp, roasted peppers, garlic, olive oil, lemon and spices. Mix gently. Serve over a bed of crisp romaine lettuce.

Serves 4

Shrimp Salad

1/2 lb. cooked small or medium shrimp
1/2 cup mayonnaise
1/2 cup finely chopped celery
4 tablespoons lemon juice
1/2 tablespoon salt
1/4 teaspoon pepper

Rinse shrimp under cold tap water and let drain in colander. Place shrimp and celery in a large mixing bowl. Add lemon juice, salt, pepper and mayonnaise. Mix well.

Serve on a bed of romaine lettuce or with fresh bread.

Serves 4

Oriental Seafood Salad

1/4 lb. finely chopped imitation crab meat
1/4 lb. cooked small or medium shrimp
2 cups ready-made cole slaw mix
2 (3 oz.) packages Ramen oriental noodles, uncooked
1 cup slivered almonds
1 cup sunflower seeds
1 cup chopped scallions
1/3 cup white vinegar
2 tablespoons balsamic vinegar
1/2 cup sugar
1/2 cup vegetable oil

In a bowl, combine vinegar, oil, sugar and Ramen flavor
packets, mix well. Add imitation crab meat, shrimp,
almonds, sunflower seeds, scallions and Ramen noodles.
Mix well and refrigerate 30 minutes before serving.

Serves 8

Lobster Salad

12 oz. chopped lobster meat
1/4 cup mayonnaise
1 tablespoon sour cream
2 tablespoons chopped celery
1/4 teaspoon black pepper
Juice from 1 fresh lemon

Place lobster meat in bowl. Add mayonnaise, sour cream, celery, pepper and lemon juice. Mix well. Refrigerate 30 minutes before serving.

Serve with fresh Italian bread or crackers.

Serves 6

Salmon Salad

1 lb. salmon fillets, cooked and chilled
4 tablespoons mayonnaise
1 tablespoon sour cream
Juice from 1 fresh lemon
1/2 cup chopped celery
1/2 teaspoon black pepper

In a bowl, combine mayonnaise, sour cream, lemon juice, celery and black pepper. Mix together until creamy. Combine salmon with mixture. Gently mix thoroughly.

Serve on a bed of fresh romaine or with crackers.

Serves 4

Shrimp with Tomato & Mozzarella

4 large ripe tomatoes
6 oz. thinly sliced fresh mozzarella cheese
8 oz. cooked medium or large shrimp
1/4 teaspoon garlic powder
1/2 cup olive oil
2 tablespoons fresh chopped basil
1/4 teaspoon black pepper
2 tablespoon sliced black olives
4 tablespoons balsamic vinegar

In a mixing bowl, combine olive oil, balsamic vinegar, garlic powder, black pepper, basil, olives and shrimp. Mix well.

Place tomatoes and mozzarella cheese on a serving dish. Top with shrimp marinade.

Serve with fresh baguette bread.

Serves 4

World Famous Seafood Markets

The Fulton Fish Market
New York City

Bustling with workers since the 1800's, the Fulton Fish Market has established itself as the largest wholesale seafood market in the United States.

The original cobblestone streets still exist today at the Fulton Fish Market as they did more than a century ago.

Over 200 different varieties of seafood are sold daily at the Fulton Fish Market.

Since the 1800's, push carts and hand trucks have been utilized to transport seafood throughout the market.

Steel hooks are used to handle fish in the market .

The Fulton Fish Market is located at the foot of the famous Brooklyn Bridge.

*Years ago, seafood was packaged and transported
in wooden boxes. Today, for economical reasons,
seafood is packaged in wax cardboard cartons.*

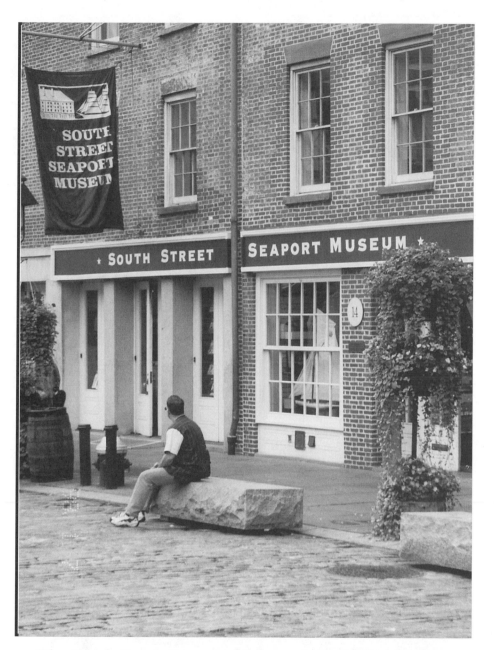

The South Street Seaport Museum includes interesting historical information about the Fulton Fish Market.

Restaurants, pubs and famous shops line the cobblestone streets of the seaport.

Little Italy
New York City

Little Italy, located less than a mile from the Fulton Fish Market, is home to some of the finest restaurants specializing in authentic Italian seafood cuisine.

Seafood prepared with a Mediterranean flair is found in the restaurants and food markets in Little Italy.

Chinatown
New York City

Located in lower Manhattan, Chinatown's fish markets thrive.

Live tilapia unloaded from fresh water tanks in Chinatown.

Live tilapia, snails, eels and dungeness crabs are several unique varieties of seafood found in Chinatown.

The Philadelphia Fish Market
Pennsylvania

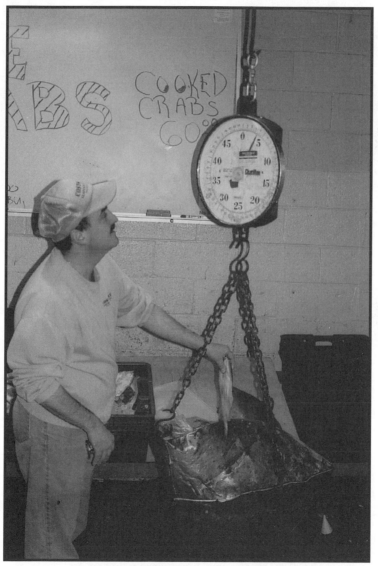

Hard-shell clams, mussels, oysters and crab are popular on menus throughout Philadelphia.

*Farmed Atlantic salmon is a popular catch at the
Philadelphia Fish Market*

The Italian Market
Philadelphia

The famous Italian Market, located on 9th and Washington Avenue offers seafood, produce, meat and other specialty foods.

Established in the early 1900's, the Italian Market began with a few street vendors selling fresh perishables from push carts.

Fishermens Wharf
San Francisco, California

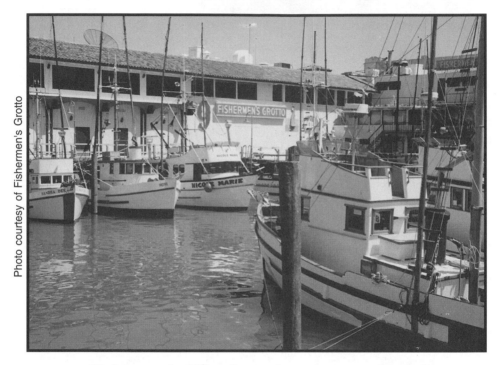

Photo courtesy of Fishermen's Grotto

*Fishermen's Wharf stands as a monumental
seaport in San Francisco, California.*

Since the early 1800's, Fishermen's Wharf has remained an active fishing port. Simple seafood stands established years ago paved the way for the elaborate seafood markets and restaurants that exist today. Fishermen's Wharf is famous for its shrimp and dungeness crab dishes.

Restaurant dining at Fishermen's Wharf offers views of Alcatraz Island and the Golden Gate Bridge.

Pike Place Market
Seattle, Washington

Photo courtesy of Pike Place Market

Surrounded by restaurants, antique shops and art galleries, the Pike Place Market in Seattle was established in 1907.

Today, Pike Place Market is a landmark offering a vast selection of seafood and other specialty foods from around the globe. Pike Place Market is one of the largest retail seafood markets in the world.

Photo courtesy of Pikes Place Market

Famous for its halibut and salmon dishes, Pike Place Market offers top-rated restaurants.

Billingsgate Fish Market
London, England

Photo courtesy of Billingsgate Fish Market

Situated in London's Docklands on over thirteen acres, Billingsgate is one of the oldest wholesale fish markets in the world.

Established in 1327 as a market which sold coal, iron, pottery, fish and other goods, Billingsgate became an exclusive fish market by the sixteenth century. Presently, Billingsgate market thrives as the center for seafood distribution in the United Kingdom.

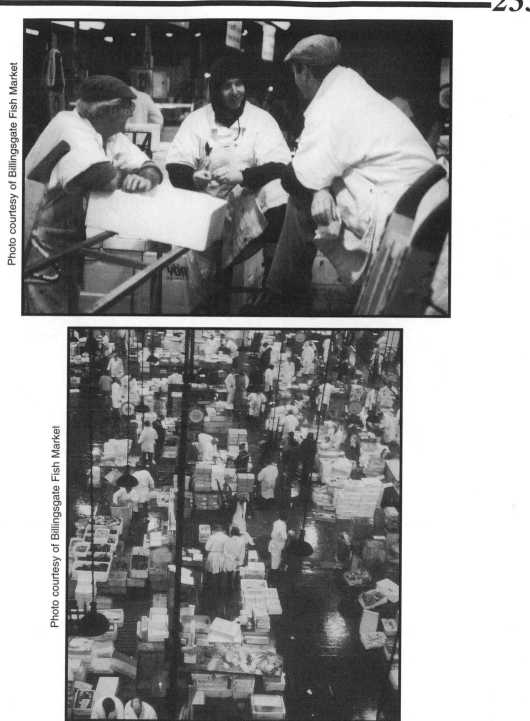

Photo courtesy of Billingsgate Fish Market

Photo courtesy of Billingsgate Fish Market

The Sydney Fish Market
Sydney, Australia

Photo courtesy of Sydney Fish Market

Located in one of the most beautiful harbors in the world, the Sydney Fish Market offers hundreds of seafood varieties including a vast array of Chinese and Thai seafood. A true fisherman's market, seafood arrives daily from the South Pacific, Asia and other parts of the world.

Using a state of the art computerized auction system, buyers complete the auction process by bidding on different types of seafood.

Famous seafood restaurants and a culinary school are located on the premises at the Sydney Fish Market.

Hong Kong Fish Market
China

Photo courtesy of the Hong Kong Fish Market

In 1945, the first wholesale fish market was established in Hong Kong. The market's objective was to improve and regulate the economics of the fishing industry. This new strategy gave consumers the opportunity to purchase a large selection of fresh seafood at reasonable prices.

Today, the Hong Kong Fish Market still offers the same high standards of quality, variety and pricing.

Tsukiji Fish Market
Tokyo, Japan

With its vast history dating back to the 1590's, the Tsukiji Market is the largest wholesale seafood market in the world. An auction process takes place each morning as buyers bid for seafood. Today, this thriving market is an integral part of Japanese daily life.

Photo courtesy of the Japan National Tourist Organization.

Photo courtesy of the Japan National Tourist Organization.

Rungis Market
Paris, France

Photo courtesy of Guinan Associates

The Rungis wholesale market located south of Paris is a major European buying center for seafood and other perishable items.

Photo courtesy of Guinan Associates

The Rungis Market is the second largest wholesale seafood market in the world.

About The Authors

Bob Marino

For many years the Marino family has been involved in the seafood business. In the early 1900's, Bob's grandfather Michael Marino, an Italian immigrant, traveled each day from Brooklyn to the Fulton Fish Market to purchase seafood for his customers.

As the tradition continued, in 1947, Bob's parent's, Gaspar and Frances, opened a fresh seafood market and restaurant in New Jersey. Today this family business is run by Bob's brother, Michael.

Bob began working in the family business at an early age, which enabled him to develop an expertise in seafood. After graduating from American University in Washington, D.C., Bob continued his education at Kean University in New Jersey, earning a Masters Degree.

Bob spent many years as a buyer/merchandiser for a supermarket chain in New Jersey. In addition, he held the position of adjunct professor at Kingsborough College in Brooklyn, New York where he lectured on seafood and marine education.

For the past decade, Bob has owned a seafood marketing company. Marino Marketing, Inc., specializes in the sale of fresh and frozen seafood. Bob's enthusiasm and desire to share his vast knowledge about seafood inspired him to write Bob & Joe's Smart Seafood Guide.

Joe D'Alessandro

At a young age, Joe D'Alessandro began working in his father's bakery where he developed a special interest in the food industry.

His grandfather established this business in 1931 when he immigrated from Italy to America. The first of its kind, D'Alessandro's, located in Montclair, New Jersey, specialized in freshly baked bread.

To help fund his college education at Montclair State College in New Jersey, Joe began working for a wholesale/retail seafood company. This experience enabled him to gain invaluable knowledge about the seafood business.

In 1982, Joe began working for a New Jersey based supermarket chain in their seafood department. As his career progressed, he became a store manager which helped him expand his expertise of the food trade.

Joe currently holds a management position in a New Jersey supermarket chain. Joe's wish to educate consumers about seafood inspired him to write Bob & Joe's Smart Seafood Guide.

Index

A

B

C

S

"Bob & Joe's tasty seafood dishes for kids are mouth
watering, I love preparing them with my Mom & Dad."
Giacomo

"Bob Marino & Joe D'Alessandro have written a delightful book about seafood that is entertaining and very informative."
Bob O'Brien, Consumer Advocate & Joe Franklin, King of Nostalgia

Bob Marino and Joe D'Alessandro
pictured on the front cover at
Marino's Grand Fish Market
in Long Island City, New York